Lecture Notes in Computer Science   13732

More information about this series at https://link.springer.com/bookseries/558

Min Luo · Liang-Jie Zhang (Eds.)

Edge Computing – EDGE 2022

6th International Conference
Held as Part of the Services Conference Federation, SCF 2022
Honolulu, HI, USA, December 10–14, 2022
Proceedings

Springer

Editors
Min Luo
Georgia Institute of Technology
Atlanta, GA, USA

Liang-Jie Zhang (ID)
Kingdee International Software Group Co., Ltd.
Shenzhen, China

ISSN 0302-9743   ISSN 1611-3349 (electronic)
Lecture Notes in Computer Science
ISBN 978-3-031-23469-9   ISBN 978-3-031-23470-5 (eBook)
https://doi.org/10.1007/978-3-031-23470-5

This Springer imprint is published by the registered company Springer Nature Switzerland AG
The registered company address is: Gewerbestrasse 11, 6330 Cham, Switzerland

Preface

The 2022 International Conference on Edge Computing (EDGE) was a prime international forum for both researchers and industry practitioners to exchange the latest fundamental advances in the state of the art and practice of edge computing, to identify emerging research topics, and to define the future of edge computing.

EDGE 2022 was one of the events of the Services Conference Federation event (SCF 2022), which had the following 10 collocated service-oriented sister conferences: the International Conference on Web Services (ICWS 2022), the International Conference on Cloud Computing (CLOUD 2022), the International Conference on Services Computing (SCC 2022), the International Conference on Big Data (BigData 2022), the International Conference on AI & Mobile Services (AIMS 2022), the International Conference on Metaverse (METAVERSE 2022), the International Conference on Internet of Things (ICIOT 2022), the International Conference on Cognitive Computing (ICCC 2022), the International Conference on Edge Computing (EDGE 2022), and the International Conference on Blockchain (ICBC 2022).

This volume presents the papers accepted at EDGE 2022. It focused on the state of the art and practice of edge computing, covering localized resource sharing and connections with the cloud.

We accepted 7 papers for the proceedings. Each was reviewed and selected by at least three independent members of the Program Committee. We are pleased to thank the authors whose submissions and participation made this conference possible. We also want to express our thanks to the Organizing Committee and Program Committee members, for their dedication in helping to organize the conference and review the submissions.

December 2022   Liang-Jie Zhang

Organization

Services Conference Federation (SCF 2022)

General Chairs

Ali Arsanjani	Google, USA
Wu Chou	Essenlix, USA

Coordinating Program Chair

Liang-Jie Zhang	Kingdee International Software Group, China

CFO and International Affairs Chair

Min Luo	Georgia Tech, USA

Operation Committee

Jing Zeng	China Gridcom, China
Yishuang Ning	Tsinghua University, China
Sheng He	Tsinghua University, China

Steering Committee

Calton Pu	Georgia Tech, USA
Liang-Jie Zhang	Kingdee International Software Group, China

EDGE 2022 Program Chair

Min Luo	Georgia Tech, USA

Program Committee

Tessema Mengistu	Virginia Tech, USA
Arun Ravindran	University of North Carolina at Charlotte, USA
Midori Sugaya	Shibaura Institute of Technology, Japan
Hung-Yu Wei	National Taiwan University, Taiwan

Services Society

The Services Society (S2) is a non-profit professional organization that was created to promote worldwide research and technical collaboration in services innovations among academia and industrial professionals. Its members are volunteers from industry and academia with common interests. S2 is registered in the USA as a "501(c) organization", which means that it is an American tax-exempt nonprofit organization. S2 collaborates with other professional organizations to sponsor or co-sponsor conferences and to promote an effective services curriculum in colleges and universities. S2 initiates and promotes a "Services University" program worldwide to bridge the gap between industrial needs and university instruction.

The Services Society has formed Special Interest Groups (SIGs) to support technology- and domain-specific professional activities:

- Special Interest Group on Web Services (SIG-WS)
- Special Interest Group on Services Computing (SIG-SC)
- Special Interest Group on Services Industry (SIG-SI)
- Special Interest Group on Big Data (SIG-BD)
- Special Interest Group on Cloud Computing (SIG-CLOUD)
- Special Interest Group on Artificial Intelligence (SIG-AI)
- Special Interest Group on Edge Computing (SIG-EC)
- Special Interest Group on Cognitive Computing (SIG-CC)
- Special Interest Group on Blockchain (SIG-BC)
- Special Interest Group on Internet of Things (SIG-IOT)
- Special Interest Group on Metaverse (SIG-Metaverse)

Services Conference Federation (SCF)

As the founding member of SCF, the first International Conference on Web Services (ICWS) was held in June 2003 in Las Vegas, USA. The First International Conference on Web Services - Europe 2003 (ICWS-Europe'03) was held in Germany in October 2003. ICWS-Europe'03 was an extended event of the 2003 International Conference on Web Services (ICWS 2003) in Europe. In 2004 ICWS-Europe changed to the European Conference on Web Services (ECOWS), which was held in Erfurt, Germany.

SCF 2019 was held successfully during June 25–30, 2019 in San Diego, USA. Affected by COVID-19, SCF 2020 was held online successfully during September 18–20, 2020, and SCF 2021 was held virtually during December 10–14, 2021.

Celebrating its 20-year birthday, the 2022 Services Conference Federation (SCF 2022, https://www.icws.org) was a hybrid conference with a physical onsite in Honolulu, Hawaii, USA, satellite sessions in Shenzhen, Guangdong, China, and also online sessions for those who could not attend onsite. All virtual conference presentations were given via prerecorded videos in December 10–14, 2022 through the BigMarker Video Broadcasting Platform: https://www.bigmarker.com/series/services-conference-federati/series_summit

Just like SCF 2022, SCF 2023 will most likely be a hybrid conference with physical onsite and virtual sessions online, it will be held in September 2023.

To present a new format and to improve the impact of the conference, we are also planning an Automatic Webinar which will be presented by experts in various fields. All the invited talks will be given via prerecorded videos and will be broadcast in a live-like format recursively by two session channels during the conference period. Each invited talk will be converted into an on-demand webinar right after the conference.

In the past 19 years, the ICWS community has expanded from Web engineering innovations to scientific research for the whole services industry. Service delivery platforms have been expanded to mobile platforms, the Internet of Things, cloud computing, and edge computing. The services ecosystem has been enabled gradually, with value added and intelligence embedded through enabling technologies such as Big Data, artificial intelligence, and cognitive computing. In the coming years, all transactions involving multiple parties will be transformed to blockchain.

Based on technology trends and best practices in the field, the Services Conference Federation (SCF) will continue to serve as a forum for all services-related conferences. SCF 2022 defined the future of the new ABCDE (AI, Blockchain, Cloud, Big Data & IOT). We are very proud to announce that SCF 2023's 10 colocated theme topic conferences will all center around "services", while each will focus on exploring different themes (Web-based services, cloud-based services, Big Data-based services, services innovation lifecycles, AI-driven ubiquitous services, blockchain-driven trust service ecosystems, Metaverse services and applications, and emerging service-oriented technologies).

The 10 colocated SCF 2023 conferences will be sponsored by the Services Society, the world-leading not-for-profit organization dedicated to serving more than 30,000 services computing researchers and practitioners worldwide. A bigger platform means bigger opportunities for all volunteers, authors, and participants. Meanwhile, Springer will provide sponsorship for Best Paper Awards. All 10 conference proceedings of SCF 2023 will be published by Springer, and to date the SCF proceedings have been indexed in the ISI Conference Proceedings Citation Index (included in the Web of Science), the Engineering Index EI (Compendex and Inspec databases), DBLP, Google Scholar, IO-Port, MathSciNet, Scopus, and ZbMath.

SCF 2023 will continue to leverage the invented Conference Blockchain Model (CBM) to innovate the organizing practices for all 10 conferences. Senior researchers in the field are welcome to submit proposals to serve as CBM ambassadors for individual conferences.

SCF 2023 Events

The 2023 edition of the Services Conference Federation (SCF) will include 10 service-oriented conferences: ICWS, CLOUD, SCC, BigData Congress, AIMS, METAVERSE, ICIOT, EDGE, ICCC and ICBC.

The 2023 International Conference on Web Services (ICWS 2023, http://icws.org/2023) will be the flagship theme-topic conference for Web-centric services, enabling technologies and applications.

The 2023 International Conference on Cloud Computing (CLOUD 2023, http://thecloudcomputing.org/2023) will be the flagship theme-topic conference for resource sharing, utility-like usage models, IaaS, PaaS, and SaaS.

The 2023 International Conference on Big Data (BigData 2023, http://bigdatacongress.org/2023) will be the theme-topic conference for data sourcing, data processing, data analysis, data-driven decision-making, and data-centric applications.

The 2023 International Conference on Services Computing (SCC 2023, http://thescc.org/2023) will be the flagship theme-topic conference for leveraging the latest computing technologies to design, develop, deploy, operate, manage, modernize, and redesign business services.

The 2023 International Conference on AI & Mobile Services (AIMS 2023, http://ai1000.org/2023) will be a theme-topic conference for artificial intelligence, neural networks, machine learning, training data sets, AI scenarios, AI delivery channels, and AI supporting infrastructures, as well as mobile Internet services. AIMS will bring AI to mobile devices and other channels.

The 2023 International Conference on Metaverse (Metaverse 2023, http://www.metaverse1000.org/2023) will focus on innovations of the services industry, including financial services, education services, transportation services, energy services, government services, manufacturing services, consulting services, and other industry services.

The 2023 International Conference on Cognitive Computing (ICCC 2023, http://thecognitivecomputing.org/2023) will focus on leveraging the latest computing technologies to simulate, model, implement, and realize cognitive sensing and brain operating systems.

The 2023 International Conference on Internet of Things (ICIOT 2023, http://iciot.org/2023) will focus on the science, technology, and applications of IOT device innovations as well as IOT services in various solution scenarios.

The 2023 International Conference on Edge Computing (EDGE 2023, http://the edgecomputing.org/2023) will be a theme-topic conference for leveraging the latest computing technologies to enable localized device connections, edge gateways, edge applications, edge-cloud interactions, edge-user experiences, and edge business models.

The 2023 International Conference on Blockchain (ICBC 2023, http://blockc hain1000.org/2023) will concentrate on all aspects of blockchain, including digital currencies, distributed application development, industry-specific blockchains, public blockchains, community blockchains, private blockchains, blockchain-based services, and enabling technologies.

Contents

Fast Offloading of Accelerator Task over Network with Hardware Assistance

Shogo Saito(✉), Kei Fujimoto, Masashi Kaneko, and Akinori Shiraga

NTT Network Innovation Center, NTT Corporation, Musashino-shi, Tokyo, Japan
{shogo.saito.ac, kei.fujimoto.rg, masashi.kaneko.dr,
akinori.shiraga.hm}@hco.ntt.co.jp

Abstract. Today, applications such as image recognition in vehicles and drones requiring high computational performance and low latency offload some tasks to accelerators. To simplify devices that provide those services, there are ways to offload the tasks to edge servers in a remote data center via a network. However, to offload the tasks over a network, data needs to be packetized and transported via a network, resulting in longer latency. Thus, we design and implement a system that enables low-latency offloading of user device tasks to a remote server via a network with the assistance of hardware functions implemented in a field programmable gate array (FPGA) on a network interface card (NIC). The FPGA-NIC and a dedicated lightweight protocol accelerate the offload processes of network transfer and data recombination in the remote server. Performance evaluations indicate the proposed system can reduce offloading latency by 55% compared with a simple method that uses a network protocol stack provided by Linux kernel.

Keywords: FPGA · Network · Accelerators · Low latency · Offloading · Smart NIC · Realtime system · Edge computing · DMA

1 Introduction

Applications that require high real-time and high processing performance have become increasingly common, such as image recognition in autonomous vehicles and drones. Because central processing units (CPUs) are not suitable for highly parallel operations such as image processing and inference processing, graphic processing units (GPUs) and field programmable gate arrays (FPGAs) are used to process them for high-speed and high-efficiency operations. However, user devices should be as simple as possible due to their portability and battery capacity imposed by energy constraints. For this reason, there are works on deploying high-performance CPUs and accelerators on edge servers in a remote data center (DC) and offloading heavy tasks of the user device to them over a network [1]. For example, in the use case of video analysis from a camera mounted on a drone, it is difficult to install a high-performance accelerator because the drone is small in size and requires power savings in terms of battery life. In this case, one

M. Luo and L.-J. Zhang (Eds.): EDGE 2022, LNCS 13732, pp. 1–17, 2022.
https://doi.org/10.1007/978-3-031-23470-5_1

approach is to offload the tasks to a server equipped with an accelerator at the edge data center. This architecture eliminates the need for a specific processor or accelerator in the user device, allowing for simplification, smaller size, lower power consumption, and longer battery life in the user device. However, offloading the tasks to a remote server over a network requires additional functions, such as network transfer and data recombination, which increase latency. Therefore, the remote-offloading systems should meet the following three requirements. The first is (a) low latency. Offloading to a remote accelerator requires additional processing, such as splitting data into packets, performing network processing by a network protocol, and recombining data again. The additional delay time due to these additional functions should be as small as possible. The second is (b) a small impact on existing applications. From the perspective of application-developer friendliness and existing applications, tasks should be offloaded over a network without making any application changes. The third is (c) no need for special hardware for offloading in user devices. User devices have limited size, and power consumption capability, so dedicated hardware for offloading is difficult to install in many cases. Note that servers in a DC can be equipped with dedicated hardware since they have lower power supply and size constraints than user devices.

We designed and implemented a remote-offloading system that enables low-latency offloading of user device tasks to a edge computing resource via a network with the assist of hardware-assisted functions implemented in a field programmable gate array (FPGA) on a network interface card (NIC). Middleware software on the user device offloads tasks to the remote server without modifying an existing application (meeting requirement (b)). It does not require special hardware in the user device (meeting requirement (c)). To meet the requirement (a), the FPGA-NIC accelerates offloading processes such as network transfers, data recombination, and data copy to a computational accelerator. In addition, a dedicated lightweight offload transfer protocol achieves faster hardware-assisted data recombination.

The rest of this paper is organized as follows. To design a remote-offload system that meets the above three requirements, we analyzed remote-offloading methods and selected a suitable one. After that, we designed and implemented a simple prototype remote-offload system, measured the latency scale of remote offloading, and detected performance overheads (see Sect. 2 and 3). Based on the revealed overheads, we designed and implemented a low-latency remote-offload system that can improve the performance overheads with an FPGA-NIC (see Sect. 4). After that, we confirm that the proposed system achieves low latency through experiments (see Sect. 5).

2   Related Works

NVIDIA DeepStream [2] is a method of remote offloading that has logic on the application side to determine which server and which task to offload. Specifically, it is a method in which the application offloads processing to a remotely located GPU server using the *gRPC remote procedure calls protocol*. This method requires the application developer to consider the logic of selecting the tasks and servers to which to offload. These considerations of the application developer do not satisfy requirement (b).

rCUDA [3] and *VOCL* [4] are methods of remote offloading with middleware that transfer memory data of functions over the network. This middleware provides compatible interfaces to standard libraries such as *CUDA* [5], and *OpenCL* [6], obtains its arguments and memory data from the application, and sends them to the remote servers over a network. This offloading is performed outside of the application, so the application does not require modification and satisfies requirement (b). These methods use message passing interface(MPI), transmission control protocol (TCP), user datagram protocol (UDP), and internet protocol (IP) in offloading over the network and use standard Linux protocol stacks and socket interfaces. Linux protocol stacks and socket interfaces orient toward generality and have high latency due to interrupt contention and unnecessary memory copying. Thus, these methods do not satisfy requirement (a).

rCUDA with Infiniband [7] uses *Infiniband* NIC and remote direct memory access (RDMA) to accelerate transfer processing. As with the rCUDA mentioned above, the middleware sends memory data and arguments of functions to a remote server for offloading. By using RDMA to send and receive data over the network, the hardware directly handles data communication and copying to host memory, eliminating protocol stack processing by software and achieving high-throughput and low-latency transfers. RDMA handles data communication and copying to host memory, which eliminates protocol stack processing by software and achieves high-throughput and low-latency transfers. This method uses *Infiniband* and RDMA to achieve high bandwidth and low latency. However, it also uses dedicated hardware to parse the RDMA protocol and transfers data directly to the host server's memory. Thus clients and servers require dedicated hardware, so this method does not satisfy requirement (c).

In remote offloading with RDMA, *Soft RoCE* enables RDMA processing in software without a dedicated NIC. According to an evaluation by *Abbasi* et al. [8], *Soft RoCE*'s latency is relatively high for hard-RoCE since *Soft-RoCE* uses the operating system (OS) driver and its overhead is added, and that does not satisfy requirement (a).

Dolphin Express [9] encapsulates *PCI Express* [10] packets with a dedicated protocol and performs parsing processing at dedicated host-adaptor cards on client and server sides, enabling *PCI Express* to long-length by switching. This mechanism enables hosts that have no accelerators to offload tasks to an accelerator on another remote machine via this switching. *NEC ExpEther* [11] encapsulates *PCI Express* [10] packets with ether frames and performs parsing at dedicated interface cards, enabling remote devices to be used with *PCI Express*. This mechanism can also offload tasks from a host that does not have an accelerator to an accelerator on a remote server. These methods require a special network interface card in both the server and the client. Thus, they do not satisfy requirement (c).

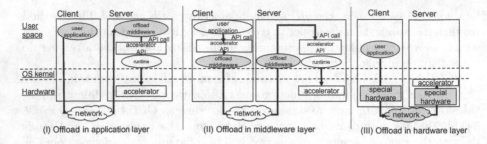

Fig. 1. Categorization of remote offloading architectures

Corundum [12] is an open-source FPGA-based network interface card and software development platform that provides various protocol stacks on FPGA-NICs to accelerate network processing. The scope of acceleration using these FPGA-NICs covers protocol processing and data transfer to the host. It does not consider offload latency to general-purpose accelerators, which is the target of this study and does not meet the requirement (a). Specifically, remote-offloading of accelerator tasks requires the ability to split and combine the task of the accelerator into multiple packets according to maximum transmission unit (MTU) and the need to offload that data to the accelerator at high speed, which are not considered in this work.

3   Analysis for Bottlenecks of Remote-Offloading Models

We take three steps to design and implement a system for low-latency offloading of accelerator tasks over a network. First, we classify existing models of remote offloading. Second, we select a suitable model that can satisfy the requirements. Third, we design, implement, and conduct a preliminary evaluation with the selected model to assess the performance and extract overheads to be solved.

3.1   Analysis for Models of Offloading over Network

In remote offloading, the client of the offloading system must transfer offloading tasks to a remote server. There are three categories, depending on where a function to transfer an offloading task is: transferring on (I) an application layer, (II) a middleware layer, and (III) a hardware layer. Figure 1 shows an overview of these three categories.

The first model transfers offloading tasks at (I) the application layer. An application needs to identify tasks to be offloaded and determine to which server to offload. Thus, application developers need to implement those functions in the application. *NVIDIA DeepStream* [2] is in this category. This model requires the logic of remote offloading for applications, so requirement (b) is not satisfied. This model satisfies requirement (c) because the offloading task could be performed with software only, and dedicated hardware is unnecessary. Whether requirement (a) is satisfied is implementation-dependent since it depends on the offloading method in the application. From these, this model can satisfy requirements (a) and (c) but not (b).

The second model transfers offloading tasks at (II) the middleware layer. Offloading to accelerators often uses a set of libraries such as *CUDA* and *OpenCL*, which we refer to as middleware in this paper. This method identifies offloading tasks with an interface of remote-offloading middleware for accelerator offloading and transferring data over a network. The applications are designed to use middleware for accelerators such as *CUDA* and *OpenCL*. This remote-offloading middleware provides a compatible interface with the existing middleware, such as the same function name and formats of arguments. When the application uses an interface of the middleware for remote offloading, the middleware provides the same interface to original middleware such as *CUDA* and *OpenCL*, so the application does not need to be modified for remote offloading. The middleware sends the task to a remote server via a network, and accelerators on the remote server compute it. After that, the client receives the result of accelerator processing and returns the value to the application. *rCUDA* [3] and *BlastFunction* [13] are in this category. This model satisfies (b) because the transfer is performed at the middleware layer, and user applications do not need to be modified. Since the user device transfers the offloading tasks by the middleware software, any special hardware for offloading is unnecessary, which enables requirement (c) to be satisfied. Like model (I), whether this model satisfies requirement (a) depends on the implementation of data transfer in the middleware software. From these, this model can satisfy all requirements if (a) is satisfied. Further investigation is required to determine the fulfillment of requirement (a).

The third model transfers offloading tasks at (III) the hardware layer. This method abstracts and lengthens a bus such as PCI Express with dedicated hardware. *Dolphin Express* [9] and *NEC ExpEther* [11] are in this category. This method enables operating systems and applications to use remote accelerators as if they were locally connected. This method provides the same interfaces to an OS and an application as locally connected accelerators, so there is no necessary for modification of the application. Thus, it can satisfy requirement (b). However, this method needs dedicated hardware on both the server and client sides. So this method can not satisfy requirement (c).

Of these three methods, offloading at (II) the middleware layer is the only one that can satisfy the three requirements. However, as mentioned above, the latency of model (II) varies depending on the transfer method and an implementation method. Thus, an additional evaluation is required to check the satisfaction of requirement (a).

3.2 Preliminary Evaluation of Offloading

To determine the latency scale of the model (II), we designed and implemented a simple prototype system and conducted a pre-evaluation.

3.2.1 Design and Implement Offloading Prototype System

We designed and implemented a simple remote-offloading system that is categorized as the model (II). Figure 2 shows the overview of the architecture. The client-side middleware receives offload tasks from a user application and transfers them via a network protocol stack of a Linux kernel to the remote server. The remote server receives the tasks that are divided by MTU size through a network protocol stack. The remote server combines them and transfers them to a server application in userland, offloading them to the accelerator. After that, the accelerator processes the task, and the middleware receives the result. The server application sends the results to the client over a network. We used the network protocol stack of the Linux kernel because it is the most widely used for network transfers. We used user datagram protocol and internet protocol (UDP/IP) as a transferring protocol between the client and server because it is simple and easy to use to measure characteristics of transferring latency. For networks where packet loss is expected, transmission control protocol and internet protocol (TCP/IP) should be used. However, it is not suitable for simple transfer time measurement due to TCP window size adjustment, retransmissions, and other logic, so we used UDP/IP in this case. For an offloading protocol, we designed an original offloading protocol on top of UDP/IP. Each packet has an 8-byte header that includes an identifier (ID) and number of max packets to identify the last packet of task transferring. The server's remote-offloading middleware can detect the order of packets with these fields in handling reordering packets.

For an experimental environment, we use two nodes: client and server machines. Table 1 shows the specifications of each machine. We set the MTU size as 1500 bytes; this is the standard size on the Internet. To evaluate the performance and identify the overhead of remote offloading, we used *OpenCL* [6] standard libraries for an application to measure its performance. *OpenCL*, provides a set of cross-platform application programming interfaces (API) and widely used runtimes for using accelerators. *OpenCL*'s API is fine-grained and supports general accelerator offloading methods. As an application for evaluation, we used *vector_add* [14] application since it is a simple matrix arithmetic program and can be used to test the performance of accelerator-based calculations. *vector_add* performs a simple operation to add two vectors together and returns a vector as the result of the addition. Figure 3 shows the architecture and processing flow of the *vector_add* in local execution and remote offloading. The solid line in Fig. 3 shows data of offloading task and is larger than the size of the MTU. The dashed line shows data for control purposes, such as arithmetic instructions, so the data is small and is not divided by the MTU. Each model has three steps in processing. The first is (α) transferring vector data from the application to the accelerator. In the *vector_add* program, the application transfers two vector data to the accelerator. The second step is (β) to instruct the accelerator to perform the calculation of the two vectors. In the *vector_add* program, the application instructs the accelerator to add two vector data that have already been transferred. The third is (γ) transferring the result data from the accelerator to the application. We set 1 Mbytes as the vector size, which assumes use-cases such as image recognition in self-driving cars because images with a resolution of about 1280×800 will be processed by the accelerator for

Table 1. Experimental platform specifications

	Client	Server
Machine	Dell PowerEdge R740	Dell PowerEdge R740
CPU	Intel Xeon 5118 2.3 GHz 12 core 2 CPU	Intel Xeon 5120 2.2 GHz 14 core 2 CPU
Memory	96 GB	128 GB
NIC	Intel XXV710	Intel XXV710
Kernel/OS	3.10.0-generic/CentOS 7.6	3.10.0-generic/CentOS 7.6
Accelerator	None	Intel Arria®10GX PAC

inference [15,16]. In this case, the *vector_add* application transfers 1 Mbytes vector data from the application to an accelerator twice, adds them together in the accelerator, and returns 1 Mbyte vector data from the accelerator to the application. We measured the execution time and breakdown of the application during remote offloading by processing, measured both 100 times, and obtained the average.

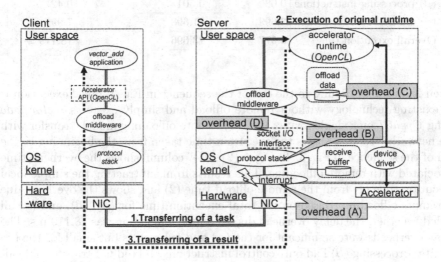

Fig. 2. Architecture of model (II) for pre-evaluation

3.3   Latency Results and Analysis for Overheads

Table 2 shows the execution time of all three steps of executing the *vector_add* program in two patterns: local offloading and remote offloading. The "(1) transfer in local" column shows the execution time in local offloading, shown in the time

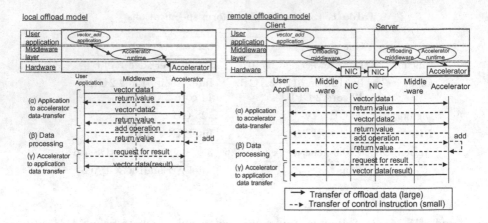

Fig. 3. Sequence of *vector_add* program in local and remote offloading

Table 2. Latency of simple remote offloading and local offloading

Step	(1) local (ms)	(2) remote offload (ms)	Gap (ms)
(α) transfer to accelerator	1.798	11.497	9.699
(β) processing instructions	0.080	0.501	0.421
(γ) transfer to application	3.699	11.698	7.999
Overall execution time	5.577	23.696	18.119

taken from the beginning to the end of the sequence in Fig. 3. Local execution is an existing technology without remote offload and simply executes *vector_add* using *OpenCL* on a single server. The "(2) remote-offloading model (transfer with the network)" column shows the execution time taken from the beginning to the end of the sequence in Fig. 3. The "gap (2) - (1)" column shows the overhead time associated with remote offloading. This results from subtracting the simple local execution time (1) from the remote-offload time (2) and shows the overhead due to remote offloading. Based on the total execution time for (α), (β), and (γ) all added together, the delay overhead due to remote offloading was 18.119 ms. The delay overheads were significant for the (α) and (γ) results but small for the (β) results. Processing (β) had only control instructions and did not transfer offloading tasks, so the packet size was small. On the other hand, processing (α) and (β) transferred the big offload data. Therefore, it was found that the latency overhead in offloading over the network occurs when transferring offloading-task. To focus on points that need improvement, we further analyze whether these occur on the server or client sides. The location of the significant delay overhead can be classified into the side of sending packets and the side of receiving packets. Larsen et al. [17] analyzed the delay time for each functional part for sending and receiving packets by the Linux kernel protocol stack. Various delay factors were presented, and among them, particularly significant delays were shown to occur on the packet receiver side for hardware interrupts, software interrupts, and socket I/O communications. In addition, Fujimoto et al. [18] also reported that packet forwarding by Linux kernel frequently occurs at the receiver side, and especially contention caused by software interrupts can cause significant delays in the order of ms. Therefore, in this paper, we first work on eliminating the delay overhead on the packet receiver side. In particular, assuming use cases such as object identification of data captured by automated vehicles and drones [15,16], since big-size data of captured images are transferred from the client to the server, significant delays will occur on the server side for packet receiving. On the other hand, after object recognition on an accelerator, the server sends the object recognition results to the client; this data is comparatively small since it is not image data but coordinate information. Thus, the delay time will be comparatively short for the client for packet receiving. Therefore, this paper focuses on speeding up the packet reception process on the server side. There are four factors in the overhead of the server-side receiving process. The first is (A) interrupt overhead. There are multiple contexts in receiving processes, such as the detection of receiving packets from the NIC triggered by a hardware interrupt, protocol processing in the kernel triggered by a soft interrupt, and protocol processing in the userland. These are executed in different contexts and cause overhead. The second is (B) packet parsing process. In the pre-evaluation configuration, the parsing of UDP/IP headers in the Linux kernel and the processing of remote-offloading protocol at the remote-offloading middleware in userspace are performed sequentially and not executed in parallel. The third is (C) the memory copy caused by the deserialization and merging of the received multiple packets. It is necessary to deserialize the header of each received packet and copy the processing target in a contiguous memory area. The server-side offloading-middleware needs to prepare a buffer for receiving packets, deserialize them and copy packets to a contiguous memory area. Larsen et al. [17] analyzed protocol processing up to Layer 4, but in remote offloading of accelerator processing, additional Layer 7 protocol processing is added, and the overhead of (B) and (C) will increase. These processes require two memory copying, and this becomes an overhead. The fourth is (D) socket I/O communications. When data divided into multiple packets is received by the socket interface, each packet causes socket I/O between the userland application and the kernel, which increases latency.

4 Proposed System and Implementation

We designed and implemented a system of the model (II) that offloads at the middleware layer via a network while satisfying requirements (a), (b), and (c). As discussed in Sect. 3, model (II) can satisfy requirements (b) and (c). However, the pre-evaluation results showed that remote offloading caused large latencies. Thus, some improvements are needed to satisfy requirement (a). As analyzed in Sect. 3.3, to reduce the overheads and faster network transfer, it is necessary to speed up to combine packets divided by MTU and offload tasks to accelerators. Software-based high-speed packet forwarding technology, such as the DPDK

[19], can only handle faster network transfers, and the overheads of recombining divided data and offloading tasks to accelerators remain. Thus, our basic idea is to implement these functions in hardware and reduce overheads. Figure 4 shows the overall architecture of the proposed system. The offload software placed in the middleware layer is installed in each client and server. This middleware transfers data for remote offloading through the network. As described in Sect. 3.3, packet processing on the server side causes significant overhead due to interrupts, memory copy, packet parsing process, and socket I/O communications. To solve this, we designed and implemented an FPGA circuit deployed in the server side that performs high-speed packet reception and processing without interrupts and processes layers 2, 3, 4, and a layer 7 remote-offloading protocol at high speed in the hardware. In addition, offload tasks divided by MTU are reassembled in the hardware, reducing socket I/O communication times. We designed a dedicated lightweight protocol and implemented it to maximize the hardware's effect of low-latency data transfer. In processing these protocol headers, we devised a unique header design that enables the processing of layers 2, 3, 4 and a special header for remoteness in parallel. Specifically, the offset in each field in the header was fixed offsets so the FPGA circuit could parse and process each in parallel.

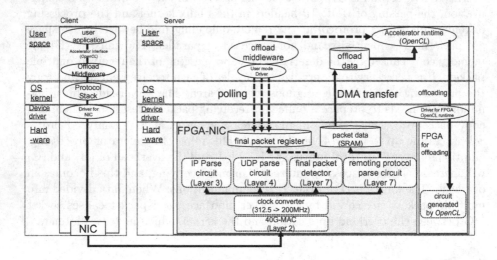

Fig. 4. Overall architecture of proposed system

4.1   Proposed System and Detailed Architecture

(1) Hardware-Based Deserializing in Server-Side FPGA-NIC. To solve the three overheads extracted in Sect. 3, we designed a parsing process in FPGA-NIC, a suitable dedicated protocol, and a method of notifying middleware of the parsing results as a low-latency-oriented functional deployment. We approach parallelizing the parsing process for each layer protocol to reduce the overhead (B) packet parsing process. To parse them in parallel, we designed dedicated hardware using an FPGA-NIC. Layers 2, 3, and 4, such as UDP/IP and Ethernet, and a dedicated header for remote offloading can be parsed in parallel by dedicated circuits in the hardware. To process them in parallel, we designed the dedicated protocols so that each layer can be processed independently (details are provided in Sect. 4.1). To reduce the overhead (C) of the memory copy caused by the deserialization and merging of the received packets, the FPGA-NIC reduces the number of data copies by processing packets in cooperation with the dedicated protocol. Layer 3 and 4 headers are not copied and are only checked inside the FPGA-NIC, and only the payload of Layer 7 is copied to host memory. The FPGA circuit uses static random access memory (SRAM) to suppress the overhead associated with the parsing process, which can be accessed with high speed to manage intermediate states. (In contrast, using dynamic random access memory (DRAM) takes time to access.) To reduce the overhead (D) of socket I/O communication, we designed the kernel to be bypassed in the data transfer to host memory. The parsing results are transferred to the memory on the host by the direct memory access (DMA) controller in the FPGA-NIC. At this time, the host CPU does not intervene to reduce overhead. To reduce the combining processing in the host memory and CPU, the FPGA-NIC calculates each packet's destination address on the host memory before transferring it via DMA. The FPGA-NIC calculates the destination memory address based on the fixed address of the packet indicated by the Layer 7 remoting protocol of each packet (details are provided in Sect. 4.1). To reduce the (A) interrupt overhead, we designed an architecture in which the completion of packet transfer is detected by polling from a userspace program. The FPGA-NIC has a register that indicates the completion of the transfer and is checked by polling from the middleware. This polling-based completion check eliminates interrupts during the transfer of each packet and the notification of transfer completion. Each protocol are parsed in parallel, and no memory copying is associated in the packet concatenation processes. These eliminate overhead (B) and (C), and there is no overhead (A) because the application detects the completion of the process by polling.

(2) Simple and Low-Latency Protocol for Remote Offloading. To handle remote-offload processing in hardware and achieve low latency, we designed a protocol suitable for hardware processing. Precisely, the offset values of each protocol header locate in a fixed address so that the parsing process of each layer can be executed in parallel to achieve low latency. We used IP and UDP as the transfer protocols for Layers 3 and 4. These protocols have a simple header, reducing the circuit size and processing time. For networks where packet loss is expected, TCP/IP can be used. We designed a dedicated protocol for the remoting protocol, Layer 7. This protocol detects the completion of packet transfer for offload and calculates the packet's destination memory address. The header contains two fields. First is number of packets divided for offload as 4 bytes, and following is a packet's offset number of divided packets as 4 bytes. The forwarding destination memory address is calculated for each packet by adding the fixed value of the packet's payload size multiplied by the packet's offset number to the first memory address set in advance in the FPGA-NIC. The FPGA-NIC also checks whether the packet is the last or not from these two fields. If the packet is the last one, the FPGA-NIC sets the final packet register on and offload middleware detects that via polling to FPGA-NIC.

(3) **Remote-offloading Library Transparent to Applications.** The transparent middleware provides interfaces to applications compatible with the existing functions for accelerators like *OpenCL*, with the same function name and argument format. This middleware provides the same interface as the existing offloading interface, such as *OpenCL* and *CUDA* runtimes, and remote offloading is handled in this middleware. As a result, an application can access a remotely located accelerator as if it is using an accelerator on the server on which it is running. Thus, in remote offloading, no modification to the application is required. The middleware on the client side has a functional part that switches between local and remote processing, and this functional part manages where the remote accelerator is located. The transparent middleware on the server side receives data at high speed via the network and inputs it to the accelerator. Combining these functions enables transparent and remote offloading of accelerator workloads. The middleware can also switch between offloading to local and remote accelerators.

4.2 Algorithm and Flow of Proposed System

The proposed system works in six steps in offloading through the network of the respective accelerator functions.

- **Step 1:** The application on the user device makes a function call, and the middleware for offloading accepts it. The function identifier, arguments, and memory area are serialized, generating data for transfer.
- **Step 2:** Serialize the data for transfer. The user device divides the memory area serialized in Step 1 into multiple packets containing remote protocols at Layer 7. These data are transferred to the server using the standard socket API.
- **Step 3:** The FPGA-NIC of the server receives the multiple packets and deserializes the Layer 2, 3, 4, and 7 protocols in parallel. When parsing this protocol, the circuit in the FPGA-NIC checks the bits in the Layer 7 remote-offloading header that indicate the final packet, and the final packet register in the FPGA-NIC is enabled. Since dedicated circuits and DMA engines execute these processes on the FPGA-NIC, memory copying by the CPU does not occur, and overheads (B) and (C) are not incurred.
- **Step 4:** The offload middleware running in the user space of the server monitors the register of the last packet in the FPGA-NIC by polling. If it detects

the last packet, it executes the offloading to the accelerator. This polling from user space detects the arrival of the final packet, and the OS kernel is not involved. Therefore, there is no interruption between the OS kernel and the user mode, and overhead (A) is not incurred.

- **Step 5:** The offload middleware on the server receives the execution results and serializes data. This serialized data is sent to the application on the user's device using the socket API.
- **Step 6:** The offload middleware on the user equipment receives the result and deserializes it. The user application obtains the function's return value and control.

4.3   Comparison Between Requirements and Proposed System

The proposed system reduces memory copies and interrupts by detecting results through hardware-based deserialization and satisfies requirement (a) low latency. From the perspective of applications, the middleware provides the same interface as the existing offloading interface, such as *OpenCL* runtimes, and remote offloading is handled in this middleware. As a result, an application can access a remotely located accelerator as if it is using an accelerator on the server on which it is running and satisfies requirement (b) a small impact on existing applications. A fixed setting can decide the server to offload by the server operator or by an external controller, and there is no effect on existing applications. This implementation submitted static settings in advance via a command line interface. Since this method uses dedicated hardware only on the server side to improve performance, the client side does not require dedicated hardware, thus satisfying requirement (c) no need for dedicated offload hardware in the user device. A demerit of this system is that it requires an FPGA-NIC on the server side, which complicates the server-side configuration.

Table 3. Experimental platform specifications

	Client	Server
Machine	Dell PowerEdge R740	Dell PowerEdge R740
CPU	Intel Xeon 5118 2.3 GHz 12core 2CPU	Intel Xeon 5120 2.2 GHz 14core 2CPU
Memory	96 GB	128 GB
NIC	Intel XL710	Intel Arria®10GX PAC
Kernel/OS	3.10.0-generic/CentOS 7.6	3.10.0-generic/CentOS 7.6
Accelerator	None	Intel Arria®10GX PAC
FPGA-NIC	None	Intel Arria®10GX PAC

5   Performance Evaluation

To evaluate the latency improvement of the proposed system, we implemented and evaluated it using actual equipment. The proposed FPGA-NIC-based remote-offloading system provides fast data transfer between client and server. Therefore, the type of operation processed by the accelerator is irrelevant in evaluating the effectiveness of the proposed system, and the data size of the task to be offloaded has an impact. Thus, the workload for the evaluation needs to be adjustable in terms of input and output data size, but the arithmetic operations can be simple. In other words, the operations processed by the accelerator, whether inference, image processing, or matrix operations, do not affect the effectiveness evaluation of the proposed system. Therefore, we use *vector_add* for the evaluation to confirm the effectiveness of the proposed FPGA-NIC accelerator, as in the pre-evaluation in Sect. 3, because *vector_add* is an application that can change the input/output size, it meets the necessary conditions for this evaluation. Since one of the target use cases of the proposed system is real-time analysis of camera images mounted on self-driving cars and drones, we analyze similarities and differences between *vector_add* and such an application in terms of characteristics of offload data transfer size. In real-time image recognition, the input data transferred to the accelerator is an image. The data returned after computation by the accelerator is assumed to be either small data such as coordinate information or image data. On the other hand, *vector_add* takes two matrix data as input and outputs one matrix data after the addition operation by the accelerator. If the input matrix data size is 1 Mbyte, the total input is two matrices and 2 Mbytes, and the output returns 1 Mbyte of data after matrix addition. Thus, the evaluation using *vector_add* can simulate to some extent the data size of the case where the image is the input and the image is the output (note that the output is half the size of the input). The case where the data of coordinates is output is difficult to simulate. However, based on the pre-evaluation results in Sect. 3, the delay time is sufficiently short when the transfer data size is small. The delay is sufficiently low, so the validation priority of the proposal is low (it is regarded as future work, as described in Sect. 6).

5.1   Evaluation Method

To evaluate the effectiveness of the proposed system, we compared the proposed system with a simple implementation of the model (II) used in Sect. 3.3. Figure 4 shows the outline diagram of the evaluation environment. Table 3 shows The server and client machine specifications of the evaluation environment. Regarding the proposed system, the server-side machine equips two FPGA cards, one of which has the hardware-based protocol processing capability described in the features of the proposed system (1). The other is an accelerator for computation offloading, similar to the one used in the pre-evaluation of Sect. 3. A 2-m cable directly connected the server and client, as in the pre-evaluation of Sect. 3, and the configuration was such that delays due to physical distance were negligible. The proposed system is a proposal to speed up the packet reception process on the server side, which speeds up the time required for (α) application-to-accelerator data transfer in Sect. 3.3 pre-evaluation. Therefore, we evaluated the delay time for (α). Data size was selected from 4 to 20 Mbytes, assuming the real-time image recognition use case. In addition to the data size of around 2 Mbytes tested in Sect. 3, we measured data as large as 20 Mbytes to see if the characteristics would change at larger sizes. The MTU size was set to 1500 bytes, standard on the Internet, as in the pre-evaluation in Sect. 3. For each data size, we took 100 measurements and averaged them.

Table 4. Latency of proposed system and pre-evaluation model

Vector size	Proposed system (ms)	Pre-evaluation (ms)	Improvement (%)
4 bytes	0.22	0.71	69.0%
1 Mbytes (equivalent to 1280 × 800 image size)	4.26	9.69	56.04%
2 Mbytes (equivalent to 1600 × 1200 image size)	8.70	19.17	54.62%
20 Mbytes (equivalent to over 4K image size)	43.95	94.53	53.51%

Table 4 compares the time of application to accelerator data-transfer as the (α) in Fig. 3. The time required to transfer data to the accelerator between the proposed system and the pre-evaluation model described in Sect. 3. For the same 1 MByte, data size as that evaluated in Sect. 3, the data transfer time (α) is reduced from 9.69 to 4.26 ms. For all other data sizes (8 Byte, 2 MBytes, 4 MBytes, 20 MBytes), the latency is reduced by about 53–56%. It can be seen that the proposed system uniformly reduces the latency to data transfer of offloading. The latency is reduced because the proposed system receives data by polling from the host CPU to the FPGA-NIC, which reduces the overhead (A) associated with interrupt processing in the server. The proposed system can deserialize UDP, IP, and the dedicated protocol header for remoteness in parallel by using a dedicated protocol and FPGA-NIC circuit design, thus reducing the overhead of (B) packet parsing process. Since the proposed system transfers the parsed results to the host memory of the server on the basis of offsets divided into multiple packets, the (C) memory copying process in the host CPU does not occur, thus reducing the overhead. It is assumed that the data receiving and protocol processing are performed independently for each packet, so the speed is not affected by the data size, and a uniform shortening effect is obtained. Note that it is desirable to evaluate a breakdown of these processing times. However, they were difficult to measure since these processes are executed at high speed and in parallel inside the hardware in the proposed system. Thus, the evaluations used the total execution time. The results of this evaluation show that the proposed system can transfer 2 MBytes of data used in image recognition with a latency overhead of 4.26 ms. In this study, the server and client are directly connected by a 2-m cable, and the configuration is such that latency caused by the network is almost negligible, but network latency must be considered in practical use. *Shanhe Yi* et al. [16] studied control methods in edge computing resources and local processing, in which the communication latency of wireless networks in offloading video processing to edge computers and the cloud was about 30–120 ms. Even with this latency, they show that offloading to the edge is effective. The overhead of 4.26 ms for offloading the accelerator processing obtained in this study is considered sufficiently small with this value. In addition, more significant time reductions are expected in future use cases where larger data sizes are transferred.

6 Conclusion and Future Work

We designed and implemented a low-latency remote-offloading system to offload tasks on a user device to an accelerator deployed in the remote server via a network. To achieve low-latency data transfer, we designed and implemented an FPGA-NIC that enables packets to be parsed in parallel, fragmented data to be recombined, and a computational accelerator to be offloaded fastly. We also designed and implemented a customized-offloading protocol that exploits the high speed of hardware support by FPGA-NICs. Performance evaluations indicate that the proposed system shortens the data transfer time by 44% compared with a system using the general network protocol stack provided by the Linux kernel.

For future work, we plan to evaluate the effectiveness of the proposed system for other applications, such as image recognition. We used UDP for simplicity in this paper, but we plan to evaluate using TCP to account for networks where packet loss is expected and detail breakdown of latencies. Furthermore, we plan to lower latency for client-side offloading-data transfer. We will perform end-to-end latency measurements assuming internet of things (IoT) devices like drones and using large-scale distributed applications to evaluate their scalability. In addition, comparisons with technologies such as Data Plane Development Kit [19], a software-based data-transfer method with low latency, are planned.

References

1. Biookaghazadeh, S., Zhao, M., Ren, F.: Are FPGAs suitable for edge computing? In: USENIX Workshop on Hot Topics in Edge Computing (HotEdge 2018) (2018)
2. NVIDIA DeepStream. https://developer.nvidia.com/deepstream-sdk
3. Duato, J., Pena, A., Silla, F., Mayo, R., Quintana-Ortí, E.: rCUDA: reducing the number of GPU-based accelerators in high performance clusters. In: 2010 HPCS, pp. 224–231 (2010)
4. Xiao, S., et al.: VOCL: an optimized environment for transparent virtualization of graphics processing units. In: 2012 Innovative Parallel Computing (InPar), pp. 1–12 (2012)

5. NVIDIA. https://developer.nvidia.com/cuda-zone
6. Khronos Group OpenCL. https://www.khronos.org/opencl/
7. Reaño, C., Silla, F., Shainer, G., Schultz, S.: Local and remote GPUs perform similar with EDR 100G InfiniBand. In: Proceedings of the Industrial Track of the 16th International Middleware Conference, pp. 1–7 (2015)
8. Abbasi, U., Bourhim, E.H., Dieye, M., Elbiaze, H.: A performance comparison of container networking alternatives. IEEE Netw. **33**(4), 178–185 (2019)
9. Krishnan, V., Miller, T., Paraison, H.: Dolphin express: a transparent approach to enhancing PCI express. In: 2007 IEEE CLUSTER, pp. 464–467 (2007)
10. PCI Express specifications. https://pcisig.com/specifications/pciexpress/
11. ExpEther Consortium. http://www.expether.org/index.html
12. Forencich, A., Snoeren, A.C., Porter, G., Papen, G.: Corundum: an open-source 100-Gbps NIC. In: 28th IEEE International Symposium on Field-Programmable Custom Computing Machines (2020)
13. Bacis, M., Brondolin, R., Santambrogio, M.D.: BlastFunction: an FPGA-as-a-service system for accelerated serverless computing. In: 2020 DATE, pp. 852–857 (2020)
14. Intel Corp, OpenCL Vector Addition Design Example. https://www.intel.com/content/www/us/en/programmable/support/support-resources/design-examples/design-software/opencl/vectoraddition.html
15. Ahmad, J., Warren, A.: FPGA based deterministic latency image acquisition and processing system for automated driving systems. In: 2018 IEEE ISCAS, pp. 1–5 (2018)
16. Yi, S., Hao, Z., Zhang, Q., Zhang, Q., Shi, W., Li, Q.: LAVEA: latency-aware video analytics on edge computing platform. In: Proceedings of the Second ACM/IEEE Symposium on Edge Computing, pp. 1–13 (2017)
17. Larsen, S., Sarangam, P., Huggahalli, R., Kulkarni, S.: Architectural breakdown of end-to-end latency in a TCP/IP network. Int. J. Parallel Prog. **37**(6), 556–571 (2009)
18. Fujimoto, K., Kaneko, M., Matsui, K., Akutsu, M.: KBP: kernel enhancements for low-latency networking for virtual machine and container without application customization. IEICE Trans. Commun. **E105.B**(5), 522–532 (2021)
19. DPDK.org. https://doc.dpdk.org/

Fair Food Delivery Trading System Based on Edge Computing and Stackelberg Game

Tao Wu[1(✉)], Xuefeng Zan[2], Lei Xu[1], Yuang Chen[1], and Kai Liu[3]

[1] Georgia Tech Shenzhen Institute, Tianjin University, Shenzhen 518055, China
taowu@gatech.edu
[2] Sun Yat-sen University, Guangzhou 510275, China
[3] Shenzhen Securities Communication Co., Ltd., Shenzhen 518040, China

Abstract. Recent years have witnessed Food-as-a-Service (FaaS) facing challenges in delivery pricing. FaaS platform collects orders from restaurants and distributes them to delivery man (DM). The fairness of the pricing and distribution have raised attention. To improve the fairness of FaaS delivery order pricing and allocation, it is critical to design a trading system with a better order distribution rule and pricing model. This paper proposes a trading system with a fair pricing model based on the edge computing system. The Stackelberg model, a second-order game model, is deployed on the edge computing system for pricing. And a smart agent algorithm based on Deep Reinforced Learning (DRL) is used for optimization. The system realizes a balance of utilities of both restaurant and DM, and it also helps the DM supply meets the spatiotemporally dynamic demands. The results indicate that the system will carry on a fair and win-win FaaS delivery trading. The verification result shows the stability of Nash equilibrium in practice and proves that our system helps build a balance between utilities of restaurant and DM. Moreover, the simulation result illustrates the system's stability and real-time response performance, and the transaction result indicates that our system helps improve market fairness.

Keywords: Stackelberg game · Dynamic pricing · Edge computing

1 Introduction

Recent years have witnessed the rapid development of Food-as-a-Service (FaaS), along with the centralization of market. Nowadays, very few companies monopolize the market in a specific area, like Meituan monopolizing the China market and GrabFood occupying the Southeast Asia market. However, due to the lack of regulation governing the business, fairness and labor relationship of the business have attracted society's attention. In this paper, we focus on delivery trading fairness between the restaurant, platform and delivery man three parties and we wish to improve the food delivery trading fairness and the labor relationship by proposing a new generation of pricing system.

In this paper, we develop a pricing system with a game-theoretic formulation, operating on the blockchain with the help of DRL for optimization. To improve the fairness of

© The Author(s), under exclusive license to Springer Nature Switzerland AG 2022
M. Luo and L.-J. Zhang (Eds.): EDGE 2022, LNCS 13732, pp. 18–31, 2022.
https://doi.org/10.1007/978-3-031-23470-5_2

the pricing model, we introduce a dynamic self-scheduling approach with the Stackelberg game model to the delivery pricing system.

For the game model, the Stackelberg game model, a second-order game model, indicates a well equilibrium. The game model realizes balanced utilities for both restaurant and DM, and the dynamic demands which are distributed spatiotemporally unbalanced is met. The blockchain is expected to check the qualification of DM before entering the market and organizes the order allocation by game model. DRL is chosen because of its efficiency for optimization.

The proposed system has the following three contributions,

1. The FaaS trading system operating on the consortium blockchain constructs a decentralized system with fog computing servers, which is open and fair, trustworthy, traceability, private and secure.
2. The second order Stackelberg game model realizes a balance between the restaurants and DM: Once receiving the order, DM's agent gives the pricing strategy at the beginning as the leader, then the restaurant reacts with the pricing strategy and give the purchase strategy.
3. Our pricing model and the order allocation system's stability can be verified by the Nash equilibrium test and the continuous order pricing and allocation simulation.

The remainder of this paper is organized as follows. Section 2 reviews related works and Sect. 3 presents the methodology. Section 4 analyzes the results from the proposed model, followed by Sect. 5, which covers an extensive discussion. Section 6 concludes the paper.

2 Related Works

The literature review will be done from the three perspectives, pricing model, takeaway food delivery pricing development and the system operation techniques.

Although price surging with dynamic multipliers is still the most popular solution in the industry [1], many novel pricing systems have been put forward, including game theorem. The game theorem is a good option because of its open and fair principle and has been deployed in many fields, including the carpooling pricing. In 2016, Li et al. proposed a carpooling trading system with a game model, which aimed to develop a dynamic pricing model considering the utilities of different passengers [2]. In 2019, Liu et al. proposed a Stackelberg Game Model to deal with Internet of Things (IoT) data trading [3]. An agent is proposed in this study to simply the multi-seller-single-user game process. The agent represents the seller side, which is the leader in the game model, and customers are the followers in the game model and decide the purchase amount based on the leader's previous price policy. Moreover, some models try to price more fairly by solving the unbalanced demand distribution. A game-theorem-based pricing model tries to identify and track the distribution of user demand for the individual social taxi, which helps release irrational pricing phenomenon by improving the cooperation efficiency of taxis [4]. Under the food delivery topic, people are just starting to use dynamic pricing model [5]. So far, little work has been performed on advanced pricing strategy application in the food delivery pricing.

Not like Software-as-a-Service or Mobility-as-a-Service, Food-as-a-Service is less used while discussing the online takeaway food order [6, 7]. However, the online food has developed greatly especially in the developing countries [8, 9]. The cheap human resource might be a potential reason for the flourishing FaaS market [10]. However, the fast-moving FaaS industry sees challenges in its labor relationship. Platforms outsource the delivery service to DMs, and there sees many conflicts between restaurants, customers and DMs [11]. The delivery pricing and order allocation fairness is one important topic needing discussion.

Computing power dramatic development supports a more efficient and economic information system, including the blockchain, Internet of Things, edge computing and cloud computing solutions [12–14]. One important reason we need edge computing and distributed system is to make a better usage of the edge computing resources, and blockchain can be used to record the usage and pay a reasonable return. Blockchain was initially a distributed ledger and then developed to carry information and trustworthy application [15], which has been introduced to the resources trading system based on the edge computing [16]. Blockchain system with debt-credit mechanism is also guaranteed by the clear systematic risk management [17], which helps improve the performance of the edge area trading. For system optimization, a smart agent based on deep reinforced learning (DRL), a novel machine-learning-approach algorithm, is widely deployed in edge computation because of its usability [17, 18]. And one author's work in the Mobility-as-a-Service trading system also provides insights in the pricing and model design [19].

3   Methodology

In this section, our model will be explained in divisions of the system:

1. Pricing model: Stackelberg game
2. Trading algorithm: DRL-based smart agent model
3. System operation: edge computing and blockchain

Furthermore, a situation statement will be given before our model.

3.1   Problem Statement

Today, FaaS is becoming more popular. Costumers order takeaway food with a mobile APP, and the platform behind the APP transmits orders to restaurant and assign DM to deliver it. To achieve the long-term interests of the business, the platform must balance utilities of 3 parties, improving their satisfaction and efficiency of the operation. The platform is also expected to regularize the trading, avoiding the conflicts between the three party. In this paper, we focus on the takeaway food delivery order pricing and allocation.

From a perspective of delivery, the outsourcing delivery market expands the potential delivery ability, so restaurants can choose the better (Normally with lower price, better feedback and shorter waiting time, as we assume that all the DMs follow the standard work rule) DM's service.

From the DM's side, he/she is trying to realize more salary by deploying a dynamic pricing system which meets the spatiotemporally dynamic customer demands. Moreover, DMs have to consider their competition as the high price may lose the order. To make the game-based pricing process more efficient, an agent operating on the blockchain is introduced as DM's intermediary trade agent. It operates the game process with the restaurant for each order on behalf of DMs, and it chooses the DM winner considering the users' utility and the supply situation.

Our expected platform operation process can be explained as follows (Fig. 1),

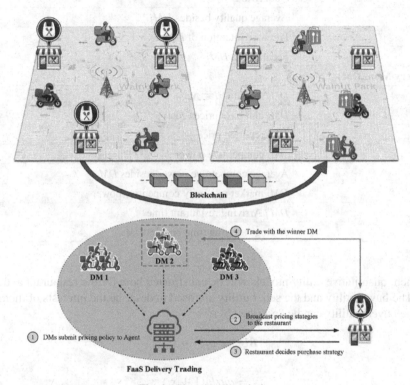

Fig. 1. Situation description

3.2 Stackelberg Game Based Pricing Model

In the hot area of the city and during the peak hours (e.g. central business district and lunch time), it is assumed that N DMs work and the set of DMs is defined as $\mathcal{N}$. Restaurants submit order delivery requests to the FaaS platform with delivery information (Table 1).

Table 1. Notation

Symbol	Definition
$\mathcal{N}$	Set of DMs
N	Number of DMs
Restaurant	
BU_i	Restaurant's utility of the trading
q_i	Quality to DM_i
$\tilde{q}_{-i}$	Average quality besides DM_i
x_i	Purchase intention of DM_i
ϑ_i	Feedback to DM_i
Delivery Man (DM)	
SU_i	DM_i's utility $\forall i \in \mathcal{N}$
c_i	DM_i unit base price (cost)
p_i	DM_i reported price
ω_i	DM_i competitive power
ω_{-i}	Average competitive power besides DM_i
π_i	DM_i market relatively competitive power
v_i	DM_i Arriving restaurant time
v_{-i}	Average arriving time besides DM_i

Then, quantitative utility models will be constructed both for the restaurant and the DM. The buyer utility and the seller utility are used to describe the interests of them.

The buyer's utility can be described by:

$$BU_i = \vartheta_i - p_i x_i \qquad (1)$$

$$\vartheta_i = q_i \alpha ln(1 + x_i) \qquad (2)$$

$$q_i = \ln\left(1 + \frac{\tilde{v}_i}{v_i}\right) \qquad (3)$$

whereas the α is a strengthen factor of feedback. As the restaurant wishes to achieve a maximum utility, the goal of optimization is:

$$\underset{x_i}{maximize}\ BU_i \qquad (4)$$

$$subject\ to\ x_i \in [0, 1], \forall i \in N \qquad (5)$$

And the Seller's utility, DM's utility, can be described as,

$$SU_i = \pi_i x_i (p_i - c_i) \tag{6}$$

$$\omega_i = \frac{q_i - \log(N)}{p_i} \tag{7}$$

$$\pi_i = \frac{\omega_i}{\frac{1}{N} \sum_{j \in N} \omega_j} \tag{8}$$

As the DM_i wishes to achieve a maximum utility, the goal of optimization is:

$$\underset{p}{maximize}\ SU \tag{9}$$

$$subject\ to\ p_i \in [c_i, p_{max}], \forall i \in \mathcal{N} \tag{10}$$

3.3 Trading Algorithm

In this section, we propose resources trading algorithm including Stackelberg game and the optimization. The resources trading algorithm includes the following steps:

1. DM_i Decides its pricing policy: $P = (p_1, p_2, \ldots, p_i, \ldots, p_N)$.
2. Restaurant decides its purchase intention based on the DM_i's pricing policy: $X = (x_1, x_2, \ldots, x_i, \ldots, x_N)$.
3. Continue the game until the change is lower than the threshold value ξ.
4. The DM's agent chooses the DM_i with maximum buyer utility as the winner.
5. The restaurant trades with winner DM_i.

The pseudocode can be described as (Table 2),

Table 2. Trading algorithm based on Stackelberg game

---

1 : **Initialize:** N DMs, M restaurant orders and Pricing policy change threshold ξ;

2 : **For each** order in M **do**

3 :   Restaurant submits order to the agent, and agent broadcasts the order to DM_i.

4 :   **Repeat:**

5 :   **Action 1**: DM_i updates the pricing strategy, $p = (p_1, p_2, ..., p_i), i \in \mathcal{N}$, to agent, and agent broadcasts price strategy p to the user (as the leader in the game).

6 :   **Action 2**: User feedbacks the purchase intention strategy, $x = (x_1, x_2, ..., x_i), i \in \mathcal{N}$, based on the price strategy p_i (as the follower in the game).

7 :   **End for** Nash equilibrium achieved:

$$\frac{\|p^{j+1} - p^j\|}{\|p^j\|} \leq \xi \tag{1}$$

8 : DM_i is chosen by:

$$\Pi = \max_{i \in \mathcal{N}}(SU_i) \tag{2}$$

9 :   The matchmaking trading between the DM winner and restaurant is made by the agent.

The agent's side optimization is done by the Deep Q-Learning Network [20]. The agent state space is defined as the restaurant's purchase intention and the price, and the action space is the price adjustment (with a little step of surging or discounting). The reward is decided by the seller utility increase due to the price adjustment.

After iterations, the price, purchase intention tends to converge and provide a stable and reasonable price as termination. The pricing policy renew, DQN reward design and the price adjustment (action space) are as follows,

$$p_i^j = d_i^j p_i^{j-1} \forall i, j \tag{13}$$

$$r_i^j = SU_i^j \left(x_i, p_i^j, p_{-i} \right) - SU_i^{j-1} \left(x_i, p_i^{j-1}, p_{-i} \right) \forall i, j \tag{14}$$

$$A_i^j = \{0.98, 0.99, 1, 1.01, 1.02\} \forall i, j \tag{15}$$

Moreover, our parameter for DQN is chosen as follows (Table 3),

Table 3. DQN parameters

Parameter	Value
Learning rate	0.005
Reward decay	0.90
ϵ − greedy	0.95
Replace target iteration	200
Memory size	8000
Batch size	56

3.4 Distributed System on Blockchain

As the FaaS delivery demand varies with time and space, individual DM cruises around the city, targeted hot areas are distributed and variable. In another word, FaaS trading happens anywhere and anytime. Thus, the distributed and efficient edge computing hardware among the city also needs a distributed software for our trading game.

To operate our trading system, our system can be deployed on a blockchain with a consensus mechanism, Practical Byzantine Fault Tolerance (PBFT). Some nodes, known as leaders in PBFT, with better computing resources, take the responsibility of keeping the ledger. Most DMs' devices are followers of PBFT, and they take orders from the trading system. The blockchain leader is elected by Proof of Work (PoW) [21].

To avoid the attack from inside and outside, only verified nodes (Including edge servers, restaurant nodes and DM nodes) are allowed to operate on the blockchain. Each node operating on the blockchain holds an account with a digital signature generated by the Elliptic Curve Digital Signature Algorithm (ECDSA). The trade is done with the unique digital account, so the transactions' security and privacy improve.

Another reason for the blockchain and distributed system is to enhance the restaurant's link to the platform and enable restaurant's digital transformation. With the return from the blockchain, restaurants will be more likely to implement the digital FaaS system and work close with the platform, which benefits to the whole industry [22].

4 Results and Analysis

In this section, results will be posted and discussed. Two results will be illustrated, Nash equilibrium verification test and the 100-order continuous simulation. Additionally, the analysis will be given attached to the result.

All computations were performed using Python 3.7.4 on a Windows environment. We used Intel(R) Core i7-8550U CPU @1.80 GHz and 16 GB of RAM, which is close to the edge node computing resource.

4.1 Nash Equilibrium Computation

Consider a scenario, 4 DMs compete for an order and their arriving time ratio is $t_{DM1}:t_{DM2}:t_{DM3}:t_{DM4} = 1:2:3:4$. Our system's maximum game iteration is set as 1500 times. The Nash equilibrium is achieved in our set iteration times and indicates a fair result in Fig. 2 and Fig. 3.

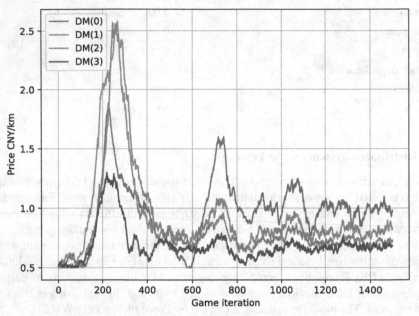

Fig. 2. Price equilibrium

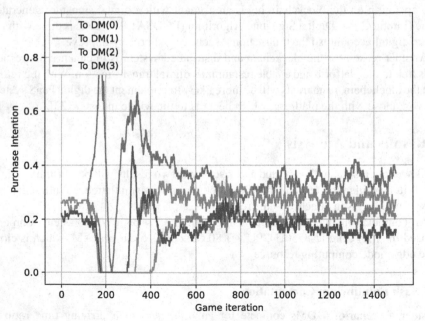

Fig. 3. Intention equilibrium

It can be seen that the fast-arriving DM has a significant advantage even if it charges for more, because it meets the food delivery's fast demand. The lead time results in the increases both in the purchase intention and the price, which protects the market's benign competition. And it sees that after 500 iterations the game converge, so we will only iterate for 500 times in the order simulation to reduce the system response time.

4.2 100-Order Continuous Simulation

In simulation, 4 groups of 100 DMs compete for orders and their arriving time ratio is $t_{DM1}:t_{DM2}:t_{DM3}:t_{DM4} = 1:2:3:4$. To show that our model with DM competitive power consideration has a stable and reasonable pricing, we compare our competitive pricing to the independent pricing game (Baseline). Each order's game iteration is limited to 500. As the order is allocated to a DM, he/she leaves the game. The purchase intention and price change over the simulation area plotted in the Fig. 4 and Fig. 5.

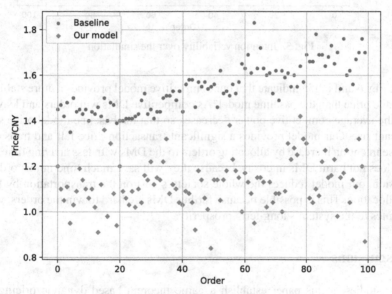

Fig. 4. Price change over the simulation

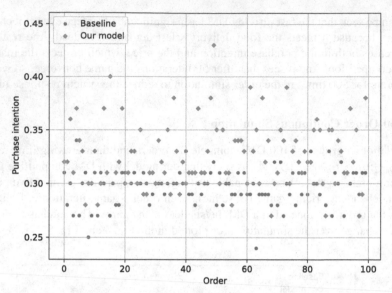

Fig. 5. Intention variability over the simulation

The Fig. 4 and Fig. 5 indicate that our competitive model provides a more stable and reasonable price than the baseline model. As competitive DMs win orders and leave the game, the average competitive power decreases so that the baseline model price sees a significant rise. Our model provides a significant transaction price fall and transaction purchase intention increase by allocating orders to the DMs with less arriving time. This action does not harm DMs interests, because they will save much time in this order. In conclusion, our model reduces the whole society's cost on the transportation by better order allocation. This is possible because farther DMs are hard to win the orders, which contributes to the system's long-term prosperity.

5 Discussions

Overall, studies in this paper establish a game theorem based dynamic pricing system which is deployable on the edge computing system. The stability of the pricing system is detailly verified, and the simulation experiment indicates the system's perfect performance. Moreover, the system does not rely on much computation, ensuring the availability of the distributed edge computation. As a result, our system is a smart combination of the edge computing hardware and the pricing game software.

Our model and result suggest a possibility of a future open FaaS delivery trading. The openness is guaranteed by the distributed system and the open consensus mechanism. Compared to the traditional center server plan, blockchain with distributed nodes provides a faster response. It saves the cost of communication with the help of edge computing nodes in the smart city.

One important future direction of the FaaS delivery trade is fairness. Only if one platform convinces its users, both DMs and restaurants, that the platform is fair can it operate its business for a long term. Our system introduces the game theorem with a clear and open policy for the pricing process. Compared to the existed surge price at the hot area plan, our plan provides a more reasonable price by introducing the interaction between restaurants and DMs to the pricing system. Thus, both restaurants and DMs do not worry about the unfair pricing due to the information gap. Our studies serve as a proof-of-concept that mobile APP makes a good use of edge computing resources.

On the other hand, the lack of real-world simulation is the main drawback of our studies, which reflects in two perspectives: lacking the order information and the limited parameters considered in our model. The real-world orders are much more complex than our simple simulation: real-world orders have different delivery requirements (e.g. different restaurants have variable requirements on delivery, including time sensitivity and weight limit) and any other potential factors not considered in our model. Thus, our model is better to verify other parameters' influence on the stability and the efficiency in the real-world order experiment. Real-world transaction experiment on the existed FaaS platform is the best choice. This experiment can be based on existing orders from the FaaS platform. Furthermore, it is also expected to carry on grayscale tests at some hot areas.

6 Conclusions and Further Work

This paper has proposed a novel FaaS trade system, possibly operating on the distributed edge computing system and blockchain. This study sets out to improve the fairness and security of FaaS trading, and the proposed system consists of dynamic pricing, order allocation and distributed ledger functions. Additionally, the smart agent with deep reinforced learning algorithm applied in the optimization provides a fast and stable convergence.

The results indicate that our system improves trading fairness in the hot area. DMs closer to the restaurant are more likely to win the game. Then, the simulation indicates our system's continuous performance. The investigation of our dynamic pricing system has shown that the game theorem deployment contributes to the fairness of the trade.

The major limitation of this study is the lack of real-world FaaS order simulation. Without real-world statistic data and test, the parameters are limited because other parameters, such as DM's reachability, are not considered because they lack knowledge of their correlation with price and purchase intention. An additional uncontrolled factor is a possibility that competition exists in the multi-FaaS-platform market.

More investigation of game theorem applied in the FaaS trade would be a fruitful area for further work. Moreover, different optimization methods are expected to be tried. More broadly, research is also needed to determine how other parameters influence the pricing and purchase decision. This work needs more understand of correlation between parameters and data support from the industry.

References

1. Cachon, G.P., Daniels, K.M., Lobel, R.: The role of surge pricing on a service platform with self-scheduling capacity. Manuf. Serv. Oper. Manag. **19**(3), 368–384 (2017)
2. Li, S., Fei, F., Ruihan, D., Yu, S., Dou, W.: A dynamic pricing method for carpooling service based on coalitional game analysis. In: 2016 IEEE 18th International Conference on High Performance Computing and Communications; IEEE 14th International Conference on Smart City; IEEE 2nd International Conference on Data Science and Systems (HPCC/SmartCity/DSS), Sydney, pp. 78–85. IEEE (2016)
3. Liu, K., Qiu, X., Chen, W., Chen, X., Zheng, Z.: Optimal pricing mechanism for data market in blockchain-enhanced internet of things. IEEE Internet Things J. **6**(6), 9748–9761 (2019)
4. Amar, H.M., Basir, O.A.: A game theoretic solution for the territory sharing problem in social taxi networks. IEEE Trans. Intell. Transp. Syst. **19**(7), 2114–2124 (2018)
5. Tong, T., Dai, H., Xiao, Q., Yan, N.: Will dynamic pricing outperform? Theoretical analysis and empirical evidence from O2O on-demand food service market. Int. J. Prod. Econ. **219**, 375–385 (2020)
6. Buckley, M., Cowan, C., McCarthy, M.: The convenience food market in Great Britain: convenience food lifestyle (CFL) segments. Appetite **49**(3), 600–617 (2007)
7. Chai, L.T., Yat, D.N.C.: Online food delivery services: making food delivery the new normal. J. Mark. Adv. Pract. **1**(1), 62–77 (2019)
8. Ren, J., et al.: Takeaway food in Chengdu, Sichuan province, China: composition and nutritional value. Asia Pac. J. Clin. Nutr. **29**(4), 883–898 (2020)
9. Habib, F.Q., Abu Dardak, R., Zakaria, S.: Consumers' preference and consumption towards fast food: evidences from Malaysia. Bus. Manag. Q. Rev. (BMQR) **2**(1), 14–27 (2011)
10. Janssen, H.G., Davies, I.G., Richardson, L.D., Stevenson, L.: Determinants of takeaway and fast food consumption: a narrative review. Nutr. Res. Rev. **31**(1), 16–34 (2018)
11. Sun, P.: Your order, their labor: an exploration of algorithms and laboring on food delivery platforms in China. Chin. J. Commun. **12**(3), 308–323 (2019)
12. Varghese, B., Wang, N., Barbhuiya, S., Kilpatrick, P., Nikolopoulos, D.S.: Challenges and opportunities in edge computing. In: 2016 IEEE International Conference on Smart Cloud (SmartCloud), New York, pp. 20–26. IEEE (2016)
13. Alamri, B., Javed, I.T., Margaria, T.: Preserving patients' privacy in medical IoT using blockchain. In: Katangur, A., Lin, S.-C., Wei, J., Yang, S., Zhang, L.-J. (eds.) EDGE 2020. LNCS, vol. 12407, pp. 103–110. Springer, Cham (2020). https://doi.org/10.1007/978-3-030-59824-2_9
14. Ramamoorthy, K.M.K., Wang, W., Sohraby, K.: Stackelberg game-theoretic spectrum allocation for QoE-Centric wireless multimedia communications. In: Zhang, T., Wei, J., Zhang, L.-J. (eds.) EDGE 2019. LNCS, vol. 11520, pp. 46–58. Springer, Cham (2019). https://doi.org/10.1007/978-3-030-23374-7_4
15. Vujičić, D., Jagodić, D., Ranđić, S.: Blockchain technology, bitcoin, and Ethereum: a brief overview. In: 2018 17th International Symposium Infoteh-Jahorina (Infoteh), East Sarajevo, Bosnia and Herzegovina, pp. 1–6. IEEE (2018)
16. Xu, C., Zhu, K., Yi, C., Wang, R.: Data pricing for blockchain-based car sharing: a stackelberg game approach. In: 2020 IEEE Global Communications Conference, GLOBECOM 2020, Taipei, pp. 1–5. IEEE (2020)
17. Liu, K., Chen, W., Zheng, Z., Li, Z., Liang, W.: A novel debt-credit mechanism for blockchain-based data-trading in internet of vehicles. IEEE Internet Things J. **6**(5), 9098–9111 (2019)
18. Mnih, V., et al.: Human-level control through deep reinforcement learning. Nature **518**(7540), 529–533 (2015). https://doi.org/10.1038/nature14236

19. Wu, T.: Consortium blockchain for secure vehicle resource trading in IoV assisted smart city: algorithms based on game theory. University of Glasgow Bachelor Dissertation, pp. 1–30 (2022)

20. Wang, Z., Schaul, T., Hessel, M., Hasselt, H., Lanctot, M., Freitas, N.: Dueling network architectures for deep reinforcement learning. In: International Conference on Machine Learning, pp. 1995–2003. PMLR, New York (2016)

21. Xu, M., Chen, X., Kou, G.: A systematic review of blockchain. Financ. Innov. **5**(1), 1–14 (2019). https://doi.org/10.1186/s40854-019-0147-z

22. Zhai, H., Yang, M., Chan, K.C.: Does digital transformation enhance a firm's performance? Evidence from China. Technol. Soc. **68**, 101841 (2022)

Thoughts on the Development of Digital Employee

Feng Liu[✉], Yishuang Ning, Xiaoquan Yu, and Maotao Zou

Kingdee Research, Kingdee International Software Group Company Limited, Wan Chai, China
vincent_lf@kingdee.com

Abstract. In recent years, the demographic dividend of the global market has gradually been exhausted. Enterprises are facing the dual pressure of labor costs and increasing pressure of market competition, and the demand for digital transformation has further expanded, with the iterative update of robotic processing automation (RPA), artificial intelligence (AI), big data and other technologies. As the most active element of the three elements of productivity, workers are also on the verge of technological explosion, and the concept of digital employee has also come into being. This paper introduces the digital employee's background, definition and key technologies, and explains the reasons and significance of the birth from a social theory perspective.

Keywords: Robotic processing automation (RPA) · Artificial intelligence (AI) · Digital employee

1 Introduction

In the past few decades, everyone has been discussing automation, including business process automation, programming automation and service automation, during which many automation technologies have been born, solving some automation scenarios in enterprises and reducing the complicated work of program developers. In recent years, with the gradual exhaustion of the demographic dividend in the global market, enterprises are facing the dual pressure of labor costs and increasing market competition, and the demand for digital transformation has further increased. The market and industry we are in now have ushered in a digital revolution, and the iterative update of technologies such as cloud computing, big data, artificial intelligence (AI) and robotic processing automation (RPA) has provided technical support for digital transformation. The concept of the digital employee is emerging. According to IDC's report in 2021, by 2024, 45% of repetitive work tasks will be automated or enhanced by the use of "digital employees" powered by AI, robotics, and robotic process automation (RPA) [1].

The digital employee is a highly anthropomorphic new type of worker created by the deep integration of multiple technologies such as "AI + RPA + Data + Robot". They exist in digital form, with avatars of human appearance, behavior, and even thoughts, capable of simulating the work of human employees, with autonomous, cognitive, and intelligent attributes. The main application areas of digital employees include banking,

M. Luo and L.-J. Zhang (Eds.): EDGE 2022, LNCS 13732, pp. 32–39, 2022.
https://doi.org/10.1007/978-3-031-23470-5_3

finance, taxation, healthcare, e-commerce, industry, manufacturing, new retail, government and other industries. In these industries, "data" is the key component, 20% of which is structured data, and for structured data, the company's approach is to use manual or some specific automation technology to process. The remaining 80% is unstructured data, which is also the focus of digital employees, using cutting-edge technologies such as AI to mine a broader data map. Therefore, analyzing and summarizing the technological development of digital employees and their impact on digital transformation can provide strong support for the digital transformation of enterprises, and at the same time, it can save human resources and operating costs, and play an important role in realizing the "last mile" of digital transformation.

The rest of this paper is summarized below. The second part introduces the key technologies related to the digital employee, and the third section is an overview of the digital employee. Finally, section IV summarizes the full text.

2   Core Technology

The essence of the digital employee is composed of RPA technology and a series of AI technologies, RPA and AI drive the development of the digital employee, and we can understand the current research status from these two directions.

2.1   RPA Technology

RPA is an abbreviation for robotic processing automation. RPA is capable of simulating human operation on a computer and is a specific software program capable of automating tasks [2]. RPA does not require any coding or programming knowledge, employees only need to be trained in how simple RPA works, and robots can be easily created through graphical user interface (GUI) and different intuitive wizards, which have advantages over traditional automation methods and can accelerate the delivery of business applications.

Currently, there are dozens of RPA vendors around the world, such as Automation Anywhere, WorkFusion, UiPth, etc. Simone Agostinelli and others compared these RPA tools and explored the forward-looking approaches needed to inject intelligence into current RPA technologies [3]. Santiago Aguirre and Alejandro Rodriguez researched RPA solutions using BPO providers as examples, and the results showed that the main benefit of RPA is increased productivity [4]. Huang F et al. explored the application of RPA in the field of auditing, demonstrating that auditors can be freed from repetitive and low-judge audit tasks [5]. Mehta R used UiPath to increase efficiency and reduce time as well as labor losses in digital marketing [6]. As the father of process mining, van der Aalst also discussed the obvious connection between RPA and process mining in 2016 [7].

2.2   AI-Related Technologies

(1) Natural language processing (NLP) technology. NLP is a key component that belongs to the digital workforce. The two main tasks of NLP are natural language

understanding (NLU) and natural language generation (NLG) [8]. NLU transforms human natural language into content that machines can understand, and NLG generates natural language that humans can understand by generating information such as machine status and notifications [9].

(2) Dialogue interaction technology. As an important capability of digital employees, conversational AI has also developed rapidly in recent years. Led by the IBM, Google, and Amazon giants, fully autonomous enterprise-class conversational robots have been developed [10]. Kepuska V, Bohouta G, et al. used a multimodal dialogue system that handles two or more combined user input modes to propose a next-generation VPA model and apply it to educational assistance, medical care, and other fields [11].

(3) Knowledge graph technology. The knowledge graph is a structured relationship model that describes things in the real world and their connections are in symbolic form, Knowledge graph was first proposed by Google in 2012, and is an important branch of artificial intelligence. Through the knowledge graph, logical reasoning can be carried out to improve the cognitive intelligence ability of digital employees. Ali Hur, Naeem Janjua, et al. commented on the latest automation techniques for building knowledge graphs and proposed research questions that need to be solved in the future [12].

3   Digital Employee

3.1   Basic Concept

According to sociological theory, productivity is the ultimate driving force for social development, and the progress and development of human society cannot be separated from the improvement and change of productive forces. Productivity also includes laborers, objects of labor, and labor tools [13]. From the perspective of the historical process, we have experienced three industrial revolutions. The first industrial revolution is marked by the steam engine as the representative of the power machine, the second industrial revolution led mankind into the electric age, and the third industrial revolution took electronic computers, atomic energy, space technology and biological engineering invention and application as the main symbol. The common denominator of these three industrial revolutions is the creation of new labor tools and labor objects, which greatly liberates the productive forces of society and promotes the development of society.

At present, with the innovation and development of artificial intelligence and automation technology, a new round of global scientific and technological revolution is being nurtured and risen. As the most active element of the three elements of productivity, workers are also on the verge of a technological explosion. The concept of the digital employee has also emerged. The digital employee is a software-based worker which constitutes a part of the enterprise workforce. It does not need office space, will not get sick, and can work 7 * 24 h. The work direction of human employees can be shifted to more specialized tasks, further improving the overall business efficiency of the enterprise [14].

3.2 Development

Today, many businesses or organizations are constantly looking for new ways to increase their digital level to improve existing business processes, meet customer expectations, and reduce costs and risks. At a time when traditional approaches were falling into bottlenecks, RPA emerged and enterprises began to adopt it as a tool to optimize their business processes. Many RPA manufacturers also refer to their products as digital robots, virtual employees, and even digital employees. This statement can be said to be both correct and incorrect. As shown in Fig. 1, the development of a digital workforce can be divided into three phases:

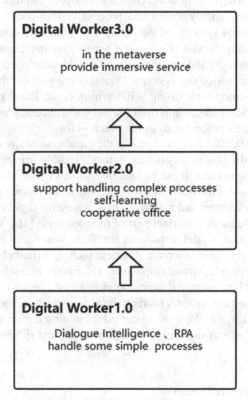

Fig. 1. The three stages of development

(1) Digital Worker 1.0. This stage is also the one where the digital employee is currently located. Based on RPA and some simple AI to build digital employees, digital employees at this stage are mainly processed for a single business process of enterprises or organizations. These digital employees cannot be completely separated from manual intervention, but can fully or semi-automatically complete a simple business process or a link in the process, and also can assist enterprise employees to quickly deal with daily rules, repetitive and process-oriented work [6], and improve

the work efficiency by dozens of times with an accuracy rate of nearly 100%. However, it cannot cope with complex business scenarios and irregular business data, and it cannot be applied to processes that need to be judged based on subjective cognition. If the process changes, it needs to be redeveloped and deployed, and the application scenarios are limited.

(2) Digital Worker 2.0. The digital workforce is also evolving in this direction. At this stage, RPA is still the core of the digital employee, deeply combined with image recognition [15], natural language processing, big data, knowledge graph and other artificial intelligence technologies to empower digital employees with perception (language, human-computer interaction, vision) and cognitive (intelligent decision-making) capabilities. Digital employees can link various systems of the enterprise, and quickly access and process various data resources based not invading the original systems of the enterprise; Eliminate system silos, and data silos, while avoiding the risk of operating across systems. Digital employees have powerful replicable capabilities that can be quickly deployed in large quantities across business scenarios and systems. Digital employees combine machine learning and deep learning with strong self-learning capabilities. It can continuously learn from historical tasks to improve efficiency and accuracy, and at the same time dig up new business processes from files such as logs.

(3) Digital Worker 3.0. 2021 is the first year of the metaverse. Major technology companies have invested a lot of money in this century's gambling, Facebook even changed its company name to meta, it can be said that whoever controls the entrance to the metaverse will master the ticket to the future world. At this stage, we have entered an environment of virtual and real symbiosis, where the digital workforce is made up of powerful AI as an important part of the metaverse [16]. When we work and live in the metaverse, digital employees are likely to serve as a public resource to us unknowingly provide immersive services, such as virtual idols, virtual anchors [17], virtual tool people, virtual employees, etc. Future technology companies will act as digital employee manufacturers, providing customers with digital employees covering entertainment, cultural tourism, finance, education, medical care, government affairs, and so on. We need to consider building a digital employee service and operation platform to manage a large number and different types of digital employees.

3.3 Overall Architecture Design

How to build a digital employee platform? This paper presents a typical architectural design for a digital employee, as shown in Fig. 2. The overall digital employee architecture is divided into three parts, including the digital employee business middle office, the digital employee service and operation platform, and the third-party system. The digital employee business middle office is a basic capability platform composed of RPA as the core technology and integrates AI components such as NLP, optical character recognition (OCR), automated speech recognition (ASR), and process mining. It also supports low-code or no-code approaches for building or modifying digital employees. Digital employees can link to the company's human resource (HR) system, enterprise resource plan (ERP) system, customer relationship management (CRM) system, etc., obtain data sources or services from these third-party systems, process the data or process based on their basic capabilities, and use cognitive intelligence technology to explore a broader data map. Digital employee service and operation platform are also crucial, which includes the interaction, skills, management, etc. of digital employees with the outside world, digital employees can serve multiple enterprises part-time. In addition, we also need to build a skills community for digital employees to communicate and make progress together, and enhance the self-learning and growth ability of digital employees to promote the good development of digital employees.

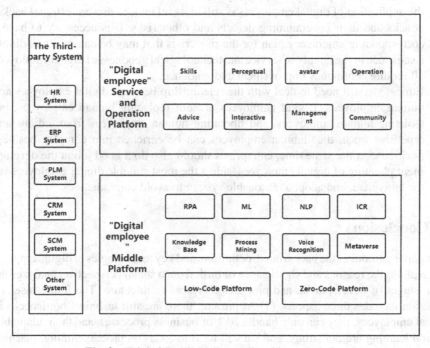

Fig. 2. "Digital Employee" overall architecture design

3.4 Existing Challenges

Although the digital employee has arrived and has been initially applied in some enterprises and fields, with very broad development prospects, we still face some problems and challenges that need to be solved.

(1) Technical bottlenecks. With the development of RPA and AI technology, there are already some manufacturers who have introduced digital employees to handle business processes through automated or semi-automated methods. However, it only solves a single business scenario of the enterprise, and for new business processes, it is necessary to redevelop and deliver the corresponding program code, which is not adaptable for learning. In various systems of the enterprise, there is a large

amount of data. According to Pareto's law, 20% of the data is structured, and our digital employees are also based on structured data for application; the remaining 80% of the data is unstructured, and we must focus on 80% of the unstructured data. We can make use of process mining, machine learning, deep learning, and other technologies to mine the value and improve the self-learning ability of digital employees.

(2) Risk. Digital workers are already starting to be used in some industries, but there are still some risks. We need to pay attention to the premise of legal compliance, to protect customer privacy and property security, especially in the financial industry, the application of digital employees is still in its infancy, to prevent external hacker attacks and their programming defects and other risks. It is necessary to have a corresponding emergency plan for the risk crisis that may be caused. In addition, issues such as the quality of service and technological goodness of digital employees all require continuous improvement and guidance.

(3) Ethics. We still need to deal with the relationship between digital employees and human employees. Digital employees are not replacing human employees, but assisting human employees, and liberating human employees from tedious and repetitive work, thus human employees can be enriched into complex business positions. At the same time, enterprises should also do a good job in the development planning of digital employees, select the most suitable digital employees for the enterprise, and adopt a reasonable system to avoid contradictions.

4   Conclusion

This paper introduces the background, definition, and key technologies of digital employees explains the reasons and significance of birth from a social perspective, analyzes the three stages of development, and proposes a typical architecture. The future research direction includes three aspects. (1) At present, there are still technical bottlenecks in digital employees, they can only handle 20% of business processes, and their adaptability and learning are not strong, and we still need to focus on process mining, machine learning, deep learning, and other technologies in the future. (2) The application of digital employees is still in its infancy, and we need to actively guard against the risks of digital employees and study how to improve system security performance. (3) We must deal with the connection between digital employees and human employees, and study the basic strategy of friendly coexistence with human employees.

Acknowledgements. This paper is supported by the Shenzhen Development and Reform Commission subject (XMHT20200105010).

References

1. Cheng, A., Lu, Y.: IDC futurescape: global artificial intelligence (AI) and automation market forecast 2022 - enlightenment from China. International Data Corporation (IDC) (2022)
2. van der Aalst, W.M.P., Bichler, M., Heinzl, A.: Robotic process automation. Bus. Inf Syst Eng. **60**(4), 269–272 (2018). https://doi.org/10.1007/s12599-018-0542-4

3. Agostinelli, S., Marrella, A., Mecella, M.: Towards intelligent robotic process automation for BPMers. arXiv preprint. arXiv:2001.00804 (2020)
4. Aguirre, S., Rodriguez, A.: Automation of a business process using robotic process automation (RPA): a case study. In: Figueroa-García, J.C., López-Santana, E.R., Villa-Ramírez, J.L., Ferro-Escobar, R. (eds.) WEA 2017. CCIS, vol. 742, pp. 65–71. Springer, Cham (2017). https://doi.org/10.1007/978-3-319-66963-2_7
5. Huang, F., Vasarhelyi, M.A.: Applying robotic process automation (RPA) in auditing: a framework. Int. J. Acc. Inf. Syst. **35**, 100433 (2019)
6. Sutipitakwong, S, Jamsri, P.: The effectiveness of RPA in fine-tuning tedious tasks. In: 2020 6th International Conference on Engineering, Applied Sciences and Technology (ICEAST). IEEE, pp. 1–4 (2020)
7. Van Der Aalst, W.: Process Mining: Data Science in Action. Springer, Heidelberg (2016)
8. Cambria, E., White, B.: Jumping NLP curves: a review of natural language processing research. IEEE Comput. Intell. Mag. **9**(2), 48–57 (2014)
9. Young, T., Hazarika, D., Poria, S., et al.: Recent trends in deep learning based natural language processing. IEEE Comput. Intell. Mag. **13**(3), 55–75 (2018)
10. Galitsky, B.: Developing Enterprise chatbots. Springer International Publishing, New York (2019)
11. Kepuska, V., Bohouta, G.: Next-generation of virtual personal assistants (microsoft cortana, apple siri, amazon alexa and google home). In: 2018 IEEE 8th Annual Computing and Communication Workshop and Conference (CCWC). IEEE, 99–103 (2018)
12. Hur, A., Janjua, N., Ahmed, M.: A survey on state-of-the-art techniques for knowledge graphs construction and challenges ahead. In: 2021 IEEE 4th International Conference on Artificial Intelligence and Knowledge Engineering (AIKE). IEEE, 99–103 (2021)
13. Miller, R.W.: Productive forces and the forces of change: a review of Gerald A. Cohen, Karl Marx's theory of history: a defense. Philos. Rev. **90**(1), 91–117 (1981)
14. Gupta, S., Rani, S., Dixit, A.: Recent trends in automation-a study of RPA development tools. In: 2019 3rd International Conference on Recent Developments in Control, Automation & Power Engineering (RDCAPE). IEEE, 159–163 (2019)
15. Jindal, A., Amir, M.: Automatic classification of handwritten and printed text in ICR boxes. In: 2014 IEEE International Advance Computing Conference (IACC). IEEE, 1028–1032 (2014)
16. Lee, M.H., Ko, J.C.: Research on application of virtual reality technology to create metaverse podcasts. In: 2022 IEEE International Conference on Consumer Electronics-Taiwan. IEEE, 133–134 (2022)
17. Babu, M.U.A., Mohan, P.: Impact of the metaverse on the digital future: people's perspective. In: 2022 7th International Conference on Communication and Electronics Systems (ICCES). IEEE, 1576–1581 (2022)

The Application of Digital Employee in Finance

Ming Zhao[✉], Yishuang Ning, ShouYu Fang, and HuiYan Xu

Kingdee Research, Kingdee International Software Group Company Limited, Hong Kong, China
zm_zhao@kingdee.com

Abstract. Digital employee that integrates various digital technologies according to the optimization needs of specific business processes plays an important role for the digital transformation of enterprises. The purpose of digital employee is to help enterprises reduce costs and increase efficiency. Nowadays, digital employee has been widely applied in various enterprise fields including human resource, operations, purchase and supply chain management, etc. In this paper, we propose a practical architecture of digital employee in finance and introduce how digital employee can be used for saving labor costs and improving efficiency. In the 10,000 reimbursement audits tasks per month, the processing time has shortened from the original 27 days to 55 h by using digital employee, greatly improving the efficiency of financial approval and providing a positive role in promoting the transformation of digital economy.

Keywords: Digital employee · Robotic Process Automation (RPA) · Financial audit

1 Introduction

In the background of the digital economy transformation era, how to make use of the digital battle power to further improve the efficiency and creativity of enterprises has become an urgent problem. After rapid development in recent years, robotic process automation (RPA) technology has gradually transited from the original field of automated testing to the heavy, repetitive and creative work [1–3]. This seemingly irreplaceable white-collar robot to complete mental work has quietly developed rapidly in various large enterprises. At this stage, COVID-19 information filling robots, financial reconciliation robots, tax declaration robots also appear on the mainstream propaganda pages of major companies.

Expense reimbursement audit is the basic financial work of enterprises, which costs a large number of repetitive and mechanical work for many enterprises, especially for enterprises that do not integrate business system with financial system. Cross-system reimbursement audit makes the work of financial personnel cumbersome. A lot of work of employees is the invoice verification and information verification. Sometimes some negligence due to human attention will also bring errors to the reimbursement system, or some non-standard operations will trouble the follow-up financial analysis.

For enterprises, paying taxes and declaring taxes are the daily tasks of financial personnel, and the declaration personnel of the Financial Sharing Center need to declare

M. Luo and L.-J. Zhang (Eds.): EDGE 2022, LNCS 13732, pp. 40–48, 2022.
https://doi.org/10.1007/978-3-031-23470-5_4

taxes regularly. After logging in the tax declaration system, the financial personnel need to manually input the invoice information first, then fill in and submit the tax application after checking and paying the tax, finally print the tax approval form. For group enterprises with more taxpayers, the tax declaration system is independent and diverse, and the declaration personnel of the Financial Sharing Center need to frequently switch the corresponding tax platform to declare, which is extremely easy to cause misstatement and underreporting.

The use of RPA technology to accomplish the scenario requirements above has improved the efficiency of enterprises, saved significant labor costs, and greatly rescued frontline workers from heavy and uncreative work. However, RPA robots imitate human behavior by performing specific tasks programmed for them [4], and for users, RPA technology is still a fixed-scene programming process, lacking intelligent experience, and still requires manual click a runnable button or enter a commands at the console to run RPA robots, which does not provide a more flexible way to control RPA robots. Digital employees with human-like intelligence capabilities have expanded the capabilities of RPA robots. They are no longer based on RPA technology alone. They understand human intentions, answer questions, and act on behalf of humans to give them control, authority and an enhanced experience [5].

Based on the characteristics of repetitive labor, large business volume and lack of creativity in the financial field, this paper expounds the shortcomings faced by enterprises, such as rapid growth of business volume, excessive financial cost pressure, easy error in manual operation and lack of artificial intelligence (AI) ability in the existing RPA robot model, and analyzes the needs for seamless communication and cooperation between employees and RPA robots. Finally, a digital employee platform is constructed based on conversational robot technology and existing financial capabilities.

2 Related Work

RPA performs repetitive tasks in a lightweight way and has become the main driving force of digital transformation [1]. There are many RPA tools on the market and are widely used in various enterprise scenarios [7], most of which are in the financial field, because financial business naturally conforms to the characteristics of RPA's task execution, that is, it is repetitive and the number of tasks is huge. In the field of finance, RPA technology has been applied to invoice reimbursement [8], auditing [9], human resources [10] and so on.

Most scholars believe that digital employees are the expansion of RPA technology [11–13], that is, digital employees are equal to RPA + AI, RPA is the execution ability of digital employees, and AI is the brain which can make intelligent judgments on the direction of RPA execution. At the same time, it can continue to learn according to existing data sets, constantly optimize skills, so as to better realize the communication and cooperation ability between digital employees and human employees.

We believe that the skills of digital employees are not only RPA, but also any other technology, such as web application program interface (API), micro services, etc. Many financial systems provide access to web API, through which users can complete invoice queries, travel applications and so on.

3   Overall Architecture

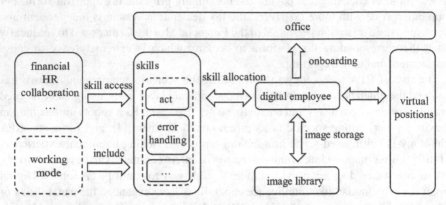

Fig. 1. The overall architecture of digital employee in Finance

Digital employee platform combines a large number of existing technologies or capabilities, including AI, third-party APIs, RPA, natural language processing (NLP), optical character recognition (OCR), etc. Using NLP technology, digital employees can communicate and collaborate with human employees in the form of dialog model to understand commands issued by human employees and execute them [14–17]. The capabilities provided by third-party API interfaces are the skills of digital employees. Digital employees can complete the task process through RPA technology or through APIs provided by third parties. Figure 1 shows the overall architecture of digital employee in finance which consists of the following five parts: office, digital employee, image library, skills, working mode. Specifically, each office has multiple virtual positions and each position can be configured with corresponding digital employee. The image library stores images of digital employees, which can be selected when creating a digital employee. The skills library includes many different skills, and each skill consists of a series of processes, including act, error handling, where different skills are oriented to different areas such as finance, HR, collaboration, etc. The working mode is a built-in operating model for digital employee to work collaboratively with human employees, which is the integration of skills, office and digital employee. For example, an employee in office uses one of the skills to complete a specific task, and such a highly uniform conceptualization mode is called the working mode of the digital employee.

3.1   Office

As shown in Fig. 1, each digital employee can be assigned different positions to join different offices, and each office contains different positions. In the field of finance, the office can be divided into expense management room, accounts receivable and payable room, fund management room, asset management room, tax management room and sharing center room according to the work content, among which the expense management room includes the following skills, namely, intelligent invoice reimbursement, intelligent voice travel reimbursement, document closure, intelligent voice travel application and other skills. Positions include reimbursement specialist and expense specialist, which can be assigned to digital employees who are assigned to their respective offices. The specific implemented technologies of skills include but are not limited to RPA, API, rule engine, image recognition, NLP and other technologies. Before using these technologies, the parameters of skills need to be configured, such as application authorization, document query condition setting and so on. Skills do not depend on the system, but can be deployed on the desktop system. For example, intelligent invoice reimbursement uses OCR technology to identify and collect invoice data through invoice system, automatically verify the authenticity, check the duplicate, verify the validity period of invoice reimbursement and whether sensitive words are compliant in the process of importing invoices and auditing, complete the intelligent filling of expense items and the intelligent judgment of deduction information, and realize accurate bookkeeping and paperless process management. The invoice system realized invoice verification, repeat verification, sensitive word verification, automatic filling in, improve reimbursement efficiency, and reduce the workload of financial approval.

3.2 Image Library

The image library is the image allocation center of digital employees, which can configure a system preset image or custom image for digital employees. A digital image includes head photo, name, age, gender, motto, status and type. Digital images can only be assigned to one digital employee at a time, that is, a digital employee has only one image.

3.3 Working Mode

The implementation of digital employees should be a mixed model [6]. A task needs the cooperation of human employees and digital employees. For example, digital employees complete a large number of repetitive and non-creative work with their extremely high efficiency and very low error rate. When they encounter operations requiring high authority in the process of execution such as account password entry, they need to inform human employees and then let them operate. To realize the hybrid working mode, digital employees need to have the ability to talk with human employees, and using conversational robotics can realize the work communication between human employees and digital employees. As shown in Fig. 2, it includes three parts: semantic parsers, selectors and skill executors. Semantic parsers understand the natural language emitted by human employees and generate the unique intention in the system; Selectors map the intention to specific office, digital employees and skill. Skill executors execute special operation according to the selected skill. Each skill is composed of initialization, execution, error handling and response. The initialization operation mainly completes the parameter configuration of the execution steps. For each skill, we provide a set of default parameters. When the natural language sent by human employees does not contain parameter information, the system will actively inquire, confirm the configuration information and store it. In the next same conversation scenario, the system prioritizes asking human employees if they use existing configuration information.

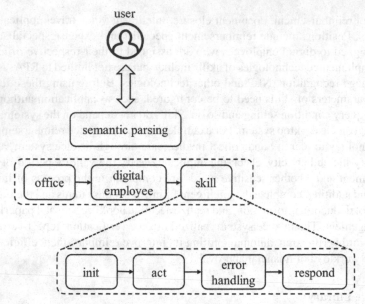

Fig. 2. Schematic diagram of digital employee operation

3.4 Skills

Execution actions are implemented by different technologies, either RPA or a mixture of web APIs or other technologies. RPA is non-intrusive, fast implementation, low learning costs, no open web API interface is still available. Various financial systems on the existing market open some services as web APIs to meet the needs of customer multi-system integration. Unlike RPA technology, Using APIs requires professional developers to write programs, which are more challenging for customers with no programming experience, but Web APIs naturally have the advantages of full accuracy, fast execution, and analyzable results. We use web APIs for simple and single-handled functions to achieve skills, such as new order functions from third-party order systems. It can be done by human employees entering order information in the operation interface and clicking the confirmation button, or by accessing the web API with key and secret and order information. If done using RPA technology, you need to enter field information in the order form several times, then click on the next cell and enter it. When the order information is very long, Keyboard input and mouse clicks are inefficient repetitive operations (just like human employees), but there are no such problems with the web API. Simply accessing the API with parameters, and reduces the number of steps and execution time.

3.5 Error Handling

Error handling is very important for enterprise business scenarios [18, 19], and some special scenarios require retries or fallbacks [20], which can cause serious errors if executed blindly and improperly. For example, digital employees use RPA technology to follow the configured steps in the tax filing page, when the operating system pops up a notification bar in the lower right corner. If the notification bar is clicked and opened by mistake, subsequent operations will not be performed correctly and effectively, and other applications may be executed incorrectly. When digital employees encounter exceptions or errors in the process of execution, they decide how to handle or revert based on the error handling mechanism of the skill itself, then generate corresponding error data and convert it into uniform format error information for downstream module use (respond). Similar to try-catch in programming languages, error handling for each skill consists of a catch and handling section, which executes specific handling when the corresponding exception or error is caught.

4 Application

Using the web API, RPA, OCR and other capabilities provided by the existing third-party system, we have built a digital employee system in the financial field, and implemented the finance-related expense management office, the accounts receivable and payable office, the fund management office, etc. One of the skills of expense management is intelligent invoice reimbursement. In a large enterprise, invoice reimbursement business has the characteristics of large quantity and repetition [21]. There are a large number of employees submitting reimbursement applications every time [22]. The quality of the reimbursement system determines the efficiency of an enterprise itself. Through the existing invoice reimbursement system, the system uses OCR technology to identify and collect invoice data, automatically verify the validity period of invoice reimbursement, check the validity period of invoice reimbursement, check the compliance of sensitive words in the process of importing invoices, complete intelligent filling-in of fee items, intelligent judgment of deduction information, and realize accurate accounting and paperless process management, and reduce the workload of financial approval.

As shown in Fig. 3, human employees and digital employees should work together to complete the reimbursement audit. In the general reimbursement audit process, the roles of human employees include: direct leader, financial examiner and financial cashier. In the original reimbursement audit process, the import and verification of invoices are operated by human employees. These work costs are not creative and can be handed over to digital employees to complete. As shown in Fig. 4, after the digital employees complete the corresponding audit work, the audit information is sent to the corresponding human auditor (or after accumulating a certain amount, the audit information is aggregated and sent again), and the human employee finally decides whether to approve it. If it refuses to pass, the applicant will be notified through the digital employee to modify the application form and submit it again.

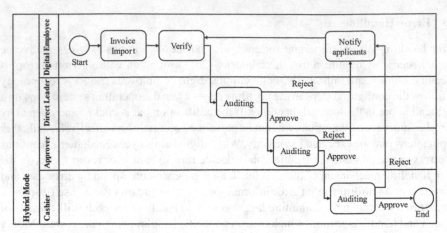

Fig. 3. Reimbursement approval process

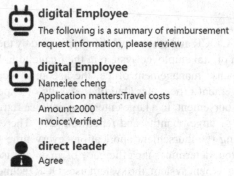

digital Employee
The following is a summary of reimbursement request information, please review

digital Employee
Name:lee cheng
Application matters:Travel costs
Amount:2000
Invoice:Verified

direct leader
Agree

Fig. 4. Reimbursement audit dialogue between digital employees and direct leaders

The invoice verification in the original review work takes an average of 1.5 min[1]. There are a large number of invoice management systems in the market, which can prevent repeated reimbursement, sensitive word verification, information filling, etc. Employees can complete it only by simple operation. According to their experience, it takes about 2 to 3 min. Through the cooperation of human employees and digital employees, it takes only 5 s for the information filling in the invoice verification to be completed by digital employees, while other operations are also reduced from a minimum of 2 min to 15 s, which greatly improves the audit efficiency. In some large enterprises, employees submit various reimbursement applications every day, such as travel expense reimbursement, software service expense reimbursement and so on. In the case of a huge amount of audit, the saved labor cost is very considerable. Assuming that there are 10000 reimbursement applications per month in the enterprise, it takes

---

[1] It takes an average of 1.5 min to open the invoice verification website(https://inv-veri.chinatax.gov.cn/index.html) and enter the ticket information after testing.

about 28 days to complete these approvals manually, while it takes only 55 h after using digital employees.

Tax declaration can also be completed by using a digital employee with RPA skills, the digital employee login in the tax declaration system, automatically fills in invoice information and submits tax application, then checks the amount declared and pays it, and finally prints the tax approval forms. When there are many tax subjects in group enterprises and the tax declaration system is independent and diverse, the original human employee operation needs to switch back and forth between multiple different systems, which takes a lot of time and may be omitted. After using digital employees, all operations are executed by RPA robots, which greatly improves the efficiency of tax declaration, and the average time of tax declaration is reduced from 30 min to 3 min.

5 Conclusion

We use various existing technologies including web API, RPA, OCR, etc. to build a digital employee platform. Each digital employee is assigned to a different office which consists of the corresponding skills, and uses conversational robots to communicate with human employees, so as to realize the demand of enterprises for further improvement of business efficiency and creativity under the background of digital economy transformation. It saves a lot of human resources and economic costs in the financial field, and provides a positive role in promoting the transformation to a digital economy.

Acknowledgements. This paper is supported by the Shenzhen Development and Reform Commission subject (XMHT20200105010).

References

1. Van der Aalst, W.M.P., Bichler, M., Heinzl, A.: Robotic process automation. Bus. Inf. Syst. Eng. **60**(4), 269–272 (2018)
2. Kaya, C.T., Türkyılmaz, M., Birol, B.: Impact of RPA technologies on accounting systems. Muhasebe ve Finansman Dergisi **82** (2019)
3. Aguirre, S., Rodriguez, A.: Automation of a business process using robotic process automation (RPA): a case study. In: Workshop on Engineering Applications, pp. 65-71. Springer, Cham (2017).https://doi.org/10.1007/978-3-319-66963-2_7
4. Automation digital worker - China l IBM. https://www.ibm.com/cn-zh/automation/digital-worker. IBM (2022)
5. How To Choose Your Digital Worker Automation Platform l Forrester. https://www.forrester.com/report/How-To-Choose-Your-Digital-Worker-Automation-Platform/RES160615.   Forrester (2022)
6. Muthusamy, V., Unuvar, M., Völzer, H., et al.: Do's and Don'ts for Human and Digital Worker Integration. arXiv preprint arXiv:2010.07738 (2020)
7. Agostinelli, S., Marrella, A., Mecella, M.: Research challenges for intelligent robotic process automation. In: International Conference on Business Process Management, pp. 12–18. Springer, Cham (2019). https://doi.org/10.1007/978-3-030-37453-2_2
8. Carden, L., Maldonado, T., Brace, C., et al.: Robotics process automation at TECHSERV: an implementation case study. J. Inf. Technol. Teach. Cases **9**(2), 72–79 (2019)

9. Cooper, L.A., Holderness, D.K., Jr., Sorensen, T.L., et al.: Robotic process automation in public accounting. Account. Horiz. **33**(4), 15–35 (2019)
10. Papageorgiou, D.: Transforming the HR function through robotic process automation. Benefits Q. **34**(2), 27–30 (2018)
11. Chakraborti, T., Isahagian, V., Khalaf, R., et al.: From robotic process automation to intelligent process automation. In: International Conference on Business Process Management, pp. 215–228. Springer, Cham (2020). https://doi.org/10.1007/978-3-030-58779-6_15
12. Zhang, C.: Intelligent process automation in audit. J. Emerg. Technol. Acc. **16**(2), 69–88 (2019)
13. Smeets, M., Erhard, R., Kaußler, T.: Looking to the future—the further development of RPA technology. In: Robotic Process Automation (RPA) in the Financial Sector, pp. 137-141. Springer, Wiesbaden (2021). https://doi.org/10.1007/978-3-658-32974-7_9
14. Galitsky, B.: Developing Enterprise Chatbots. Springer, Cham (2019)
15. Frommert, C., Häfner, A., Friedrich, J., et al.: Using chatbots to assist communication in collaborative networks. In: Working Conference on Virtual Enterprises, pp. 257–265. Springer, Cham (2018). https://doi.org/10.1007/978-3-319-99127-6_22
16. Li, T.J.J., Radensky, M., Jia, J., et al.: Interactive task and concept learning from natural language instructions and gui demonstrations. arXiv preprint arXiv:1909.00031 (2019)
17. Li, T.J.J.: Multi-modal interactive task learning from demonstrations and natural language instructions. In: Adjunct Publication of the 33rd Annual ACM Symposium on User Interface Software and Technology, pp. 162–168 (2020)
18. Casati, F., Cugola, G.: Error handling in process support systems. In: Advances in Exception Handling Techniques, pp. 251-270. Springer, Berlin (2001). https://doi.org/10.1007/3-540-45407-1_16
19. Bohus, D., Rudnicky, A.: Error handling in the RavenClaw dialog management architecture. In: Proceedings of Human Language Technology Conference and Conference on Empirical Methods in Natural Language Processing, pp. 225–232 (2005)
20. Chandra, A., Bossen, D.C.: Time-lag duplexing-a fault tolerance technique for online transaction processing systems. In: Proceedings Pacific Rim International Symposium on Fault-Tolerant Systems, pp. 202–207. IEEE (1997)
21. Zheng, S.: Financial management innovation of electric power enterprises based on robotic process automation. In: 3rd International Seminar on Education Innovation and Economic Management (SEIEM 2018), pp. 207-210. Atlantis Press (2019)
22. Czernin, J., Phelps, M.E.: Positron emission tomography scanning: current and future applications. Annu. Rev. Med. **53**, 89 (2002)

The Significance of a Second-Person Perspective for the Development of Humanoid AI

Hanlin Ma[✉] [iD]

Suzhou University of Science and Technology, Suzhou, China
fanfan2011cn2000@gmail.com

Abstract. Anthropocentrism and non-anthropocentrism are a pair of basic directions in cognitive science and AI research. These directions correspond respectively to "first person" and "third person". The confrontation between these two concepts not only has guiding significance for the exploration of cognitive science but also has ethical importance. Human-like AI (for instance, Artificial General Intelligence, AGI for short) research hovers between them. I propose a second-person, or limited consensus perspective as a philosophical and ethical research context that is integrated with the first and third person to constitute a "trinity" relationship—what I call the "trinity of the contexts of intelligent artificiality", which could be represented by the relationship between emulation, simulation, and imitation. The consequences of the general loss of the first-person context will be explored, including the uncertainty of the ethical landscape of humankind—such as the fragmentation of the self—and the risk of going against the original intention of AGI research. This cannot be fixed by returning to a first-person perspective. The second-person context is an idea that is situated between anthropocentrism and non-anthropocentrism, and it may be employed to avoid these risks.

Keywords: Imitation · Second-person perspective · Anthropocentrism · Non-anthropocentrism

1 Introduction

A recent episode that highlighting the topic of humanoid AI is the story of Google's "The language Model for Dialogue Application (LaMDA)". A test engineer, Blake Lemoine claims that this chatbot system displays sentience and even "wants" to be respected. Including Google, probably most of the AI researchers would not share any consensus with Blake Lemoine. Microsoft Chief Data Scientist Juan M. Lavista Ferres says: "LaMDA is just a very big language model with 137B parameters and pre-trained on 1.56T words of public dialog data and web text. It looks like a human because is trained on human data". One reason why people don't believe it has evolved sentient AI is that the framework contains no intention of creating a self-cognitive structure.

Building something that "acts like a human" actually has not been the main goal in the AI industry recently, even though it always catches the attention of the public. This phenomenon shows that the humanoid AI standard inspired by Turing Test does not

M. Luo and L.-J. Zhang (Eds.): EDGE 2022, LNCS 13732, pp. 49–63, 2022.
https://doi.org/10.1007/978-3-031-23470-5_5

get agreement from the realm of industry. This may be caused by the fact that making a Humanoid AI has been largely abandoned by most scientists. Even though LaMDA talks like a human who seems to know who it is, it still is considered a coincidental emulation.

Nowadays, researchers in the realm of Artificial General Intelligence (AGI) are working on another direction in making humanoid AI – to design or produce a humanoid cognitive structure. But would this kind of AI simulation necessarily become an existence that could get along with real human beings, given the case that it probably does not physically look like a human in any way nor have a life that is anything like a human being's If AGI was like this, then the research into social AI would appear redundant. Philosophically speaking, when we focus on social AGI research, not just normal social AI study, merely staying with the idea of emulation and simulation is not enough, the introduction of the concept of imitation from the Theory of Mind could be a productive avenue to explore.

2   The Definitions of Emulation, Simulation, and Imitation

Please consider the following three cases:

1. When I mimic my cat's meow, he does not react to me.
2. The team of Markram (2015), which is affiliated with the Human Brain Project (HBP), builds "a digital reconstruction and simulation of the anatomy and physiology of neocortical microcircuitry that reproduces an array of in vitro and in vivo experiments without parameter tuning and suggests that cellular and synaptic mechanisms can dynamically reconfigure the state of the network to support diverse information processing strategies" (Markram et al. 2015).
3. . One of the most influential primate researchers, Tetsuro Matsuzawa, can "speak chimp" with his experimental subjects. On BBC Earth's YouTube channel, you can see a video of him greeting the chimpanzees and getting responses.

In case 1, I present an action called emulation, by which I wish my cat would subjectively believe that I am communicating with him by presuming that my consciousness is similar to his. I do not know what I precisely express, however. In this case, I am trying to build a "sense of another mind" in my cat's mind, which is first person. Besides, the picture of my mind in his mind is also presumed to be judged as the first person. However, I fail.

In case 2, the HBP team processes a digital simulation of a mouse brain by reconstructing the physiology of neocortical microcircuitry. Nevertheless, the simulation can be oriented to other varieties of cognition, rather than staying with physicalism only. According to the introduction by Kotseruba and Tsotsos (2020), there are at least 195 different cognitive architectures featured in 17 sources in the last 40 years. All of these architectures could be implemented in AI applications. However, except for the model of HTM (hierarchical temporal memory; see Hawkins and Blakeslee 2004), which shares the elementary philosophical background of intelligence with HBP, there are lots of different styles of cognitive architectures that can be simulated, such as EPIC (Kieras 2017), represented by a symbolic system, ACT-R (Anderson and Lebiere 2003), Soar

(Laird et al. 1987) featured as hybrid systems, etc. They are platforms to represent the access consciousness (A-consciousness) of Block (1995).

Comparing case 1 with case 2, in case 1, my emulation was committed to eliciting a first-person belief in another mind, namely that I have a phenomenal consciousness (P-consciousness). In case 2, the simulations for cognitive research were committed to establishing a series of third-person cognitive states that can serve any available purpose, e.g., to represent the behavior of greeting. All inner informational structures of these cognitive states can be shared, replicated, and re-established. However, let us consider case 3, in which Tetsuro Matsuzawa interacts with chimps by imitating them. He knows the meaning of his chimpanzees' roar and how the chimps would react to his imitation.

The understanding of what was represented by case 1, case 2, and case 3 can share the same series of actions from different perspectives. By drawing a parellel with the cover illustration of Gödel, Escher, Bach: An Eternal Golden Braid (Hofstadter 1979), I exhibit my expression of the relationship between emulation in case 1, simulation in case 2, and imitation in case 3 in Fig. 1. This shows that they cannot be reduced to each other, but rather represent different aspects of one individual process, which I call the "trinity of the contexts of intelligent artificiality" (TCIA). Nevertheless, having different understandings determines which direction we are heading in when we realize human minds through computers. In other words, when we use the first person (context of emulation), the third person (context of simulation), or the second person (context of imitation) as the pivot to construct a certain value parameter in the development of AI, we will face different ethical and other meaningful implications. My suggestion is to choose the context of the second-person perspective. The most important reason is that different perspectives represent different understandings and standards for agents. In Sect. 2, I will indicate that in the realm of HCI (human-computer interaction), the pivotal status of the context of emulation—or what I call Turingism—has been arrogated by the context of affordance, which may cause the fragmentation of self. In addition, unlike the operation of HCI, the research into artificial general intelligence (AGI) is supposed to explore the essence of self, while the contagion from the context of affordance could affect any neutral context of simulation, including AGI research. In Sect. 3, my concern goes toward the profound ethical significance of simulation proposed by Floridi (2013). I will charge his theory with a dilemma, then suggest a second-person context to explore AGI, which is neither anthropocentric nor non-anthropocentric.

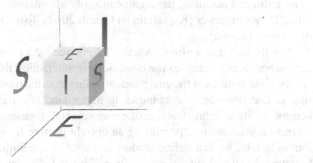

Fig. 1. .

3 Abandoned Emulation

Although emulation, simulation, and imitation may partly share features as behaviors, their intentions are entirely dissimilar in the sense of practical goals. Let us start with emulation. According to Merriam Webster's Dictionary, emulation means "ambition or endeavor to equal or excel others (as in achievement)". Accordingly, behavioral emulation is a kind of "endeavor to equal action" that aims to achieve behavioral sequences or goal-oriented behaviors. In a way, the Turing Test shows a typical example of the emulation of human actions, which tricks a person into believing that they are talking to a human (Turing 1950). This means that Turingism is typically anthropomorphic. Moreover, the ELIZA effect proves that people will unconsciously and emotionally respond to the ELIZA computer conversation program by ascribing a human mentality to it (Weizenbaum 1966). Since the ELIZA effect or something similar (Seibt, Nørskov, and Hakli 2014) make it possible to obtain available feedback from humans, anthropomorphization becomes an aspired destination in the realm of social robots (Duffy 2003). On the other hand, the "Uncanny Valley" (Mori et al. 2012) proves that some emulations may not deploy desirable anthropomorphization, even producing uncomfortable feelings in experimental participants. Therefore, avoiding uncanny robotic design appears to be a theme of HCI. Currently, from an HCI point of view, it seems that whether people believe that robots are "thinking" is not the crucial issue. Rather, fitting their cognitive or social expectations for specific situation of interaction is concerned. How to manipulate human perception to adapt to the interface design has become a hot research topic in HCI and social robotics (Vallverdú et al. 2016).

Has research in the area of AI and human interaction directed by Turingism been abandoned? If so, for what reason? The answer to the first question is yes. The philosophy of HCI only borrows the appearance of Turingism by embracing the idea that participants are thought of as perceiving the interface or "behavior of the system", as if they are demonstrating some features or capacities of intelligence. In fact, in HCI, the important thing is how participants respond to the interface of the system, not what they consciously believe about the system. The underlying idea here may not involve total behaviorism, but is close enough. Most HCI research revolves around the conception of affordance, which can be used as the foundation of our analyses. This term was initially proposed by Gibson (2014) within his ecological approach to perception. It was introduced to HCI by Norman (1988) and quickly became a widely accepted keyword among researchers. Due to its unlimited potential, the significance of "affordance" in HCI has been developed into different branches (Kaptelinin and Nardi 2012). To avoid confusion, I will stay with its original meaning.

Briefly, affordance almost equals "interaction". As point 5 below will demonstrate, affordance mostly refers to the conditions in interaction that emphasize living beings' abilities and features of the environment, rather than the mental or physical events occurring in that situation. For example, to understand affordance, we can imagine living beings' ability to define features of environmental situations. Just as Gibson mentioned, "stand-on-able" means "permitting an upright posture for quadrupeds and bipeds". By imitating him, we can define "radar-scan-able" as "permitting an ultrasonic reception to detect the spatial conditions for flying" for the affordance between bats and cave. It seems that affordance represents the possibility of the behavior that occurs in the inter-action between a living being and its circumstances. According to Kaptelinin and Nardi (2012), Gibson's theory of affordances can be summarized as follows:

1. Affordances are perceived directly; their perception is not based on an interpreta-tion of initially meaningless "raw" sensory data; 2. Affordances are relational properties; they emerge in the interaction between the animal and environment: the same environ-ment may offer different affordances to different animals (or humans); 3. Affordances are independent of the situational needs of the perceiver; 4. Natural environments and cultural environments should not be separated from one another; 5. The theory of affor-dances is concerned with how affordances are perceived rather than affordances per se.   .

For the convenience of analysis, let us apply the framework of affordance to Turingism. First of all, the only purpose of Turing Test deployment is to achieve specific beliefs within the human's mind by AI which emulates the human.. This concerns the perceiver's interpretation of sensory data. Second, the immediate relationship between the human and the AI in the emulation test is worthy of attention, but there is no for-mal permanent *relationship properties* to be concerned about. Furthermore, the situation with Turingism seems to be a second-order or overlapping relation. And, as perception addresser, emulation targets the perception of the addressee. This is a dimension of the second-person situation that does not involve consensus between the addresser and the addressee. The ideas described in points 4 and 5 do not apply to our current analysis.

If the practical field of Turingism is taken over by the theory of affordance, which is a radical embodied theory, then what happens subsequently? This is where my Theory 1(T1) of humanoid AI or robot development comes in:

T1. The result of affordance theory's replacement of Turingism is the split of human cognition of the self and all possible ethical consequences this brings. However, this practical problem cannot be solved through a purely theoretical return to Turingism.

The application of affordance theory to HCI is committed to controlling the uncer-tainty of the interaction. Another dissimilarity between affordance and Turingism is that the self of another mind will never be considered a cognitive object in the affording relationship. Nevertheless, the uncertainty that is driven by different types of selves and the referential psychological distance will be committed as parameters to quantify the Turingism situation.

According to Knobe and Nichols's (2011) outstanding work, three types of selves can be detected corresponding to psychological distance in idealized conditions. These are: the physical concept of the self, the psychological concept of the self, and the executive concept of the self. I am concerned with the last two. The psychological concept of the self refers to mental processes in the sense of psychology or cognitive science, which are the kinds of "mental events" that philosophers Davidson (2001) and Kim (1973) worked on. The corresponding causal relationship is mental causation. The concept of self-implementation refers to an "agent"; a similar "subject" commonly used in the history of philosophy. Its metaphysical properties are not limited by physical time and causality (in contrast to the psychological concept of the self). The corresponding causal relationship is agent causation (Clarke 1993; O'Connor 1996). Moreover, according to Construal Level Theory (CLT; see Trope and Liberman 2010), the recognition of events with a greater psychological distance is more abstract and essential (which means a high construal level); the recognition of events with a shorter psychological distance is more specific and direct (which means a low construal level). The characteristic of psychological distance is not fixed, although mainstream items are time (close or not), space (close or not), the closeness of social relationships, and real or counterfactual events.

I will use human-likeness as the parameter of psychological distance, which refers to the trends of probabilities of whether participants are more likely to treat the objective robotic interface as an agent or mental self. By employing the analysis of the "Uncanny Valley", I will clarify how the "fragmentation of human cognition of the self" in T1 happens. As Mori described, the Uncanny Valley refers to the fact that "in climbing toward the goal of making robots appear like a human, our affinity for them increases until we come to a valley, which I call the uncanny valley" (Mori et al. 2012, p. 98; Mori (1970); see Fig. 2). In the last 50 years, dozens of explanations have been posited (Wang et al. 2015). Because I am inclined to the Theory of Mind, my explanation stays with Gray and Wegner (2007, 2012). According to their experiments, participants were more likely to respond to the robotic interface as an agent rather than as an experiential sSelf. Experience is thought of as a more essentialized quality than agency, in the sense of treating robot as human-like being. Thereby, "if machines are held to be essentially lacking experience, then an appearance which suggests this capacity—i.e., human-like eyes that convey emotion (Adolphs et al. 2005)—could conflict with this expectation and therefore be unsettling" (Gray and Wegner 2012, p. 126). This explains why the Uncanny Valley occurs, but it does not mean that machines will never be treated as if they have some experience (Waytz et al. 2010), as indicated by the peak before the valley. Therefore, zoomorphic or other caricatured design appears to be useful to avoid the Uncanny Valley (Fong et al. 2003).

What I want the reader to take note of here is that to treat the object as a more experiential self does not presume that the participants are attracted by more experiential details of the object. Sometimes, a well-deployed cartoon character in the sense of affordance may be accepted as a more vivid object. By virtue of this, participants' cognition of this carton character will become a "zoom-in case", in contrast to, participants' cognition of a normal and healthy man, which will become a "zoom-out case", in which participants do not pay close attention to their objects. Accordingly, we may combine the quantification of the psychological distance of human-likeness and the psychological distance of the measure of accepted experience from the objects (y-axis in Fig. 2).

According to Knobe and Nichols (2011), at a short psychological distance (zoom-in case), "people are willing to take a thick view of what counts as the self". In this case, the average score comparison between agent self and experiential self is 4.95/5.48. At a long psychological distance zoom-out case), on the other hand, "people are inclined to think of the self as a thin executive self", and the average score comparison is: 6.10/3.95. This means that in the affordance of zoomorphic or some caricatured cases, people are more likely to treat the self of the cognitive object as an agent. The agency of the robot may not equal to the agency of humans, however. In other "zoomed-in" research of Knobe and Nichols, comparing computers as a determined cognitive process with humans, participants were more inclined to judge that no alternative possibility (AP) could be attributed to the computer. This means that participants are more likely to treat robots as controlling Selves but not agents with complete free will in the sense of libertarianism.

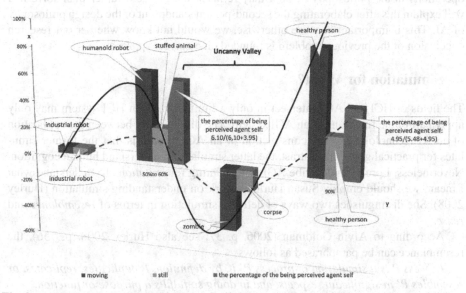

Fig. 2. x-axis represents the percentage of affinity or counterpart of the percentage of being perceived agent self, and the y-axis represents the percentage of the psychological distance of the perceiver from industrial robot to a healthy person

With the context of being trapped in the situation of designed affordance, if we follow Luciano Floridi's (2013) proposition that treating AI as a moral agent to some extent without possessing any libertarian-type free will (Kane 1998), then we will face at least two types of splits in the self: the split between the experiential self and agentic self, and the split between self with AP and controlling self. Therefore, it seems that the human HCI industry has a significant opportunity to create the type of humanoid robot with executive selves similar to humans'. Meanwhile, such selves are considered to have no passion or freedom. Furthermore, the affordance that characterize these selves may be used to eliminate some uncertainty in human life in their interaction with computers. Thanks to this, some potential evolutionary directions of memes may be eliminated. Another fact makes this conclusion look even more disquieting: due to the huge impact of modern communication methods on human society (which was catalyzed by Covid-19), the the psychological distance between people and the "psychological distance" between people and machines are becoming more and more equal. The problem here is not what the computer or any interface in that affordance has deflected in humans' cognition, but rather what future this kind of HCI would create for humans. A possible situation may be that humans will be trapped under the control of HCI, which is not a dictatorship but stronger and more effective than a dictatorship.

Another of the subsequent thought-provoking ethical problems is whether people will perceive the bullying by any kind of embodied interface in the same way as the bullying by other people. Some experimental (Keijsers 2020) or theoretical studies (Kissel 2020)

have appeared. What we should beware of, however, is that when we start research of this kind, we automatically get back to the Turingism standpoint. Nevertheless, these operations in the philosophy of HCI may re-mask the problem rather than solve it. I will explain this after elaborating the second-person standpoint of the design philosophy of AI. This is important because otherwise, we would not know whether our research conclusion of the previous problem is founded on a correct approach.

4   Simulation for What?

The fields of HCI and AGI intersect in only a limited way. An HCI system may only apply part of the functions of an AGI system. The dissimilarity between the application of an AI technology and the construction of an AGI system is that the former simulates for practical goals. In contrast, the latter simulates to understand human cognition. Nevertheless, I prefer to describe AGI as simulating for *imitation*. To understand what I mean, we should employ Susan Hurley's work on understanding simulation (Hurley 2008). She distinguishes two ways of defining simulation in terms of *resemblance* and *reuse*.

According to Alvin Goldman (2006, p. 37; see also Hurley 2008, p. 756), the resemblance can be paraphrased as follows:

Process P is a simulation of process P' if, by definition, P duplicates, replicates, or resembles P' in significant respects, and in doing so fulfills a purpose or function.

Philosophers like Bostrom (2003) and sci-fi movie directors like the Wachowskis (*The Matrix*) may share this definition when they use the concept "simulation", but they more likely agree with the scientists who posit a *theoretically driven simulation*, which is *intrapersonal* and represented in case 2 of the introduction above. According to Goldman, "A computer may simulate wind flow around a suspension bridge by applying the laws of relevant theory to derive a symbolic description or graphical representation that is about the target. It does not use or undergo the same type of processes as its target undergoes, but rather represents the target processes, using another mechanism" (Goldman 2006, pp. 35–36; see also Hurley 2008, p. 758). Evidently, all AGI researchers share this definition of simulation.

Nevertheless, when it comes to *interpersonal mindreading*, the simulation may become "reuse", in terms of appealing to the *Simulation Theory (ST)* of mindreading. As Hurley and Goldman stated, ST proponents believe that in mindreading, people ply their own mental elements to rebuild the mental state of other minds. However, there is another mindreading theory named *Theory Theory (TT)*, in which people read other minds by *interpersonal theoretically driven simulation* in the approach of theorizing the information exploited by the experience of the other agents. No matter whether ST or TT is right, they both represent an interpersonal resemblance that I name "*imitation*", similar to what Tetsuro Matsuzawa does with his chimps.

In this case, it seems that AGI designers' works are dissimilar from the landscape of the human mind described by mindreading theorists, although the latter may have a chance of being successful in the HCI field based on the former. Nevertheless, some AGI designers are not optimistic about humanoid AI. Jeff Hawkins says: "I don't believe we will build intelligent machines that act like humans, or even interact with us in human-like ways" (Hawkins and Blakeslee 2004, p. 206. The common purpose of AGI study is to probe the essence of intelligence, whose range may not be restricted to human cognition. Since not all characteristics of human intelligence are necessary, (and some may be accidental products brought about by evolution), AI researchers need only focus on the intellectual features that are rationalized by cognitive science to structure the AI system. For example, NARS (an AGI architecture designed by Wang Pei) sets emotion as a crucial feature that helps control the action selection and decision-making processes (Li et al. 2018). This setting has already exhibited an adequately human-like and rationalized theorization of emotion, even though it falls only under the intrapersonal frame. In contrast, ST scholars may disagree with it in the light of some empathic emotion, which can be explained by the mirror neuron mechanism. They may believe that sometimes people feel pain and sadness only because others' miserable situation evokes these emotions. If empathy is an automatic mechanism of humancognition, could we just ignore it, even though it has survived through the accidental process of evolution?

Through answering this question, we will find that at least part of my reason to elevate the significance of a second-person perspective on AI development is driven by ethical considerations. Here is my Theory 2:

T2. General artificial intelligence research under the third-person perspective is necessary to explore the essence of self, but if the second-person knowledge of imitation is not used for reference, AGI will probably proceed in a non-anthropocentric direction.

It is not possible to establish without any ethical contradiction an AI with a self by simulating the human mind on the one hand, while on the other hand not building a human-like contact approach with the person in the system. Newell (1994, p. 19) proposes thirteen constraints that shape the mind.

It is odd that John R. Anderson chooses to omit point 9 (the feature of social community) when he applies these principles to test his famous ACT-R system, which is partly based on Newell's AI philosophy (Anderson and Lebiere 2003). Anderson may be thinking along the same lines as Hawkins, believing that ACT-R does not need to interact with humans.

Nevertheless, another spontaneous answer is to say that if the other 12 characters have been realized, then the last one may be subsequently achieved. Then, two things may occur. The first one is that machines may develop their own social entrainment without connecting with human society. This is not just fiction. Wang Pei pictured this landscape of AI species in light of his AGI predictions at the 12th International Conference, AGI 2019. If the AI species live in a parallel dimension away from ours, then nothing ethical needs to be said about it. However, what if they would have some connection with human society? Then, "how should we deal with this situation?" will be a question. If this occurs, then what I mentioned in T1—that the problem of HCI with affordance cannot be solved through a purely theoretical return to Turingism—applies to our debate right now.

Previous research has shown that people can feel empathy for robots when the robot is mistreated (Darling et al. 2015). In an interesting study on robotic bullying, Keijsers (2020) concludes that people would apply the same mind attribution to robots and humans, because they feel unacceptability in the case of both robotic and human bullying. This is because of the empathy that participants feel toward robots. In this case, empathy is measured as a first-person perspective, thereby fitting the Turingism context. If all these conclusions make sense, then it appears that passing an empathic Turing Test may afford entrainment between humans and robots. But this will not be true, because it is possible that some AGI techniques coincidently couple the conditions of HCI affordance, and at the same time, could pass the Turing Test. Hence, the problem in T1 remains. This is why I suggest a second-person perspective in T2. For example, if we use it to analyze robotic bullying, we may reach a different conclusion. Why would the same attitude of the unacceptability of different agents certainly stem from the "same mind attribution to robots and humans"? Why would it not stem from the same mistreatment coming from the "same" human? This experiment only reveals that participants may discern part of the interpersonal situation between the human abuser and the robot victim as the normal status of their lives. It is reasonable to infer that people may agree that the abuser in this situation may bully the robot as if they were bullying some iron box, or animal, or even some fool. But will they rationally agree that the robotic victim believes itself to be suffering like a human being bullied? I think not. The analysis framework I currently use is in light of the second-person standpoint.

If an AGI system rather than just normal AI with the anthropomorphic embodied interface was meant to implement social entrainment with humans, then it has to be designed with the perspective of the second person. This means that this AGI agent will believe that they are (or are not) a human-like agent to some extent, and believe that people consider that they believe that they are (or are not) a human-like agent to some extent, and that, thanks to this consideration, people believe they are (or are not) a human-like agent to some extent, etc. There are two aspects to realizing this blueprint: one aspect is to endow robots with mindreading ability, and the second is to equip people with a proper principle of operation allowing recognition all intelligent features of AI, and then to clarify to what extent it is human-like.

I will superficially engage with the first aspect. It appears that the domain of mindreading is still a minefield between TT and ST. ST may be thought of as conveniently bridging the first-person and second-person perspective by the mechanism of mirror neurons. But what remains unexplored is how to build a mirror connection between humans and robots. If embodiment AGI like Cogprime were prompted to engage in this domain, then they would need to address T1 first. Besides, some studies relying on TT have made good progress in second-person machines. Nevertheless, the question is how to devise the inductive strategy of TT. Bello and Guarini (2010) and Bello & Bringsjord (2013) established a Polyscheme framework by virtue of CLT and cognitive logic based on possible world semantics. TT seems to be more easily accomplished in a *symbolic AI* that is adept at inductive inference. If researchers insist on absorbing empathy mechanisms into the system, then it will be a challenging work.

5 Imitation: In the Gap Between Non-anthropocentrism and Anthropocentrism

Based on the philosophy of information, Floridi (2013) designs a third-person informational ethical system, which distributes different agents using the scale of what he calls "levels of abstraction (LoA)". Different LoAs are represented by different simulations and coupled with different but comparable degrees of morality. The convenience of this theory is that it could couple AI agents with specific moral identities. From the Turingist perspective, since the robot interfaces are more likely to be treated as agents who can always precisely control their "behavior" but not as agents with free will like humans, they may not be treated as possessing responsibility, which is presumed to be coupled with legal rights. From the parlance of Floridi's philosophy, robotic agents are supposed to be endowed with a morality similar to what they possess from the Turingist perspective. Floridi however has a more ambitious plan for the continuum of all simulations. According to the reducibility between simulations or LoA, he premises that different agents could be compared in the same fundamental LoA by using a coarse-grained evaluation method. In this LoA, all the agents could be described as possessing the following capacities (Floridi 2013, p. 147):

1. To respond to environmental stimuli—for example the presence of a patient in a hospital bed—by updating their states (interactivity), for instance by recording some chosen variables concerning the patient's health. This presupposes that H and W are informed about the environment through some data-entry devices, for example some sensors; 2. To change their states according to their own transition rules and in a self-governed way, independently of environmental stimuli (autonomy), for example by taking flexible decisions based on past and new information, which modify the environmental temperature; and 3. To change the transition rules by which their states are changed according to the environment (adaptability), for example by modifying past procedures to take into account successful and unsuccessful treatments of patients. The so-called agents H and W could be morally compared by using a rule (O):

An action is said to be morally qualifiable if and only if it can cause moral good or evil, that is, if it decreases or increases the degree of metaphysical entropy in the infosphere.

Evidently, both normal AI and AGI may fit the requirements of the agent of Floridi, even though all of them could be attributed to the set of features of human free will. In a way, what Floridi does is not abandoning free will, but rather shortcutting it. By investigating the problem of free will from all aspects, we may find that it is not easy to discern a necessary and sufficient condition for free will, and we may agree that the boundary of free will is vague. However, vagueness just means incompleteness and not uselessness or meaninglessness, as Floridi believes. For example, I may ask: in what way can we call an agent "self-governed"? Could the agent in the situation of the famous Frankfurt-style stories (Frankfurt 1969) be called "self-governed"? It seems that many issues arising from the question "what does it mean to be under control?" need to be figured out before deploying point 2. Furthermore, in regard to point 3, should we not first determine the criteria for *successful and unsuccessful treatments of patients*? I think all conclusions of the debate on free will could be used as references to enrich the extension and intension of free will. Not all elements in the set of components of free will can be realized by normal AI, and that is what AGI should engage with. According to my previous statement, we may detect that Floridi treats simulations as a static set, not a dynamic developing process, which is the essence of research in AGI.

Floridi believes that as long as the interaction is analyzed under the premise of these agent theories, moral evaluation can be given. At the same time, this type of interaction shares the same extension with the interactive relationship in the context of affordance, but does not rely on any analysis of human perception. Floridi's theory and the theory of affordance share different aspects of non-anthropocentrism. Floridi's informational philosophy supports a non-anthropocentric ontology for the continuum of the relational artifact, AI, and persons. HCI, according to the philosophy of affordance, brings people into a part of a non-anthropocentric interaction.

Nevertheless, this non-anthropocentrism may face a dilemma. It seems that Floridi does not believe any ultra-intelligent machine will emerge in the future. From that, we can infer that he may not believe that a machine in the form of what Firth (1952) called the "ideal observer" will come into our world at anypoint. Since the "ideal observer" is defined by its being omniscient and omnipercipient with respect to non-ethical facts, and hence would not make moral mistakes relying on the reductionist moral philosophy, an ultra-intelligent machine like this would never cause any entropy production in our moral world. Consequently, if Floridi persists in disagreeing with this anti-existence that runs contrary to the Second Law of Thermodynamics in the sense of information or intelligence, then he will inevitably fall into a defeatism of morality, because there would be no reductive metaphysical entropy process at the elementary level of LoA or simulations. In contrast to Floridi's foundationalism, Rifkin (2009) believes that entropy reduction—what he calls empathic activity—may always happen at some high order and local kinds of simulations, and entropy reduction may cause entropy production elsewhere; in other LoA or simulations.

According to this moral theory of entropy, when we introduce the context of imitation, would an eerie landscape inspired by *The Matrix* be brought about by the second-person design philosophy of AI? I think it will not, because imitation is premised on a cross-level simulation connection, which differs from the anthropocentric theory of Rifkin. Although this connection relies on a more basic simulation, it will not provide any significance of morality or any kind of culture on that level. The significance of morality stays with the context of imitation itself, which cannot be reduced to the context of emulation and simulation. Consequently, I will move on to T3 as the end of this section:

T3. The main significance of intelligent interactionism rather than human-computer interactionism under the second-person perspective is that it connects the development of human-like intelligence research with the consensual mental content formed by human sociality. It cannot guarantee any utopian vision, but provides new possibilities for the mental development of human society. Briefly, the philosophy of the second-person perspective stems from P.F. Strawson's work (2014) on reactive attitude and is developed by Steven Darwall (2006) into a systematic theory on morality. In their view, to every individual, moral accountability should be discerned and developed in a dynamic process of predicting of others' feedback to one's own actions, and thereby regulating one's beliefs and intentions. The moral agent in this social circle will be treated as having the same moral consideration as oneself. Everyone in the social circle shares the consensual mental content by which they will reach consent. This content is not based on the requirement that every construction of self in the circle share the same LoA.

6 Conclusion

Tegmark (2017) divides the development of life into three stages, determined by life's ability to design itself:

Life 1.0 (biological stage): evolves its hardware and software. Life 2.0 (cultural stage): evolves its hardware, designs much of its software. Life 3.0 (technological stage): designs its hardware and software.

We cannot posit that this is an anthropocentric theory, but to Tegmark it appears that a higher-order life form leads to higher-order self-designing ability, which seems to be an ideal human attribute. Regardless of whether intelligence in the future will be able determine its own hardware and software, it does not surrender this power of self-determination to evolution. This idea stems from the observation that as the model of AI, human minds are able to partly determine their own development. However, if humans abandon the Turingist approach to designing machine interfaces interacting with them, rather than affording implements to modify themselves by taking advantage of their cognitive fitness, then how can humans determine their software, since many of their embodied cognitions were determined by their hardware? The goal of Turingism in the context of emulation is to let the intelligent interface be perceived as a human being, but not be comfortably perceived, as well as to pander to the perceivers' cognitive fitness. Furthermore, intelligence based on the context of affordance may easily pass some Turing Tests, although not all of them. Intelligence of this kind could possibly be realized by a simulation practice of AGI. Development in this direction seems to have little business with the task of exploring the essence of humanoid intelligence.

Perhaps proposing and emphasizing the previous challenge per se deserves further examination. Nevertheless, I offered my own suggestion for the development of humanoid AI, especially AGI. From my perspective, positing any humanoid intelligence as both moral addressor and addressee is not only a direction that *should* be taken, but also a proper simulation that may fit the real situation when humans relate with each other. Human babies have been described as imitating machines. At the early stage of human development, their growth focuses on the ability to attribute others' endogenous intentions to others' exogenous behavior as mentally sourcing as they do to themselves. The necessary and sufficient condition of the mechanism of second-person knowledge is still being explored, just as other cognitive processes of humans. Perhaps second-person knowledge research based on AGI will complement second-person research in the Theory of Mind. At the same, the direction of this approach may guarantee the ethical acceptability of AGI.

References

Adolphs, R., Gosselin, F., Buchanan, T.W., Tranel, D., Schyns, P., Damasio, A.R.J.N.: A mechanism for impaired fear recognition after amygdala damage. Nature **433**(7021), 68–72 (2005)

Anderson, J.R., Lebiere, C.: The Newell test for a theory of cognition. Behav. Brain Sci. **26**(5), 587–601 (2003)

Bello, P., Bringsjord, S.: On how to build a moral machine. Topoi **32**(2), 251–266 (2013)

Bello, P., Guarini, M.: Introspection and mindreading as mental simulation. In: Proceedings of the Annual Meeting of the Cognitive Science Society, vol. 32, no. 32 (2010)

Block, N.: On a confusion about a function of consciousness. Behav. Brain Sci. **18**, 227–287 (1995)

Bostrom, N.: Are we living in a computer simulation? Philos. Q. **53**(211), 243–255 (2003)

Clarke, R.: Toward a credible agent-causal account of free will. Noûs **27**(2), 191–203 (1993)

Darling, K., Nandy, P., Breazeal, C.: Empathic concern and the effect of stories in human-robot interaction. In: 2015 24th IEEE International Symposium on Robot and Human Interactive Communication (RO-MAN), pp. 770–775. IEEE (2015)

Darwall, S.L.: The Second-Person Standpoint: Morality, Respect, and Accountability. Harvard University Press, Cambridge (2006)

Davidson, D.: Essays on Actions and Events: Philosophical Essays, 2nd edn., vol. 1. Clarendon Press, Oxford (2001)

Duffy, B.R.: Anthropomorphism and the social robot. Robot. Auton. Syst. **42**(3–4), 177–190 (2003)

Firth, R.: Ethical absolutism and the ideal observer. Res. **12**(3), 317–345 (1952)

Floridi, L.: The Ethics of Information. Oxford University Press, Oxford (2013)

Fong, T., Nourbakhsh, I., Dautenhahn, K.: A survey of socially interactive robots. Robot. Auton. Syst. **42**(3–4), 143–166 (2003)

Frankfurt, H.G.: Alternate possibilities and moral responsibility. J. Philos. **66**(23), 829–839 (1969)

Gibson, J.J.: The Ecological Approach to Visual Perception: Classic Edition. Psychology Press, New York (2014)

Goldman, A.I.: Simulating Minds: The Philosophy, Psychology, and Neuroscience of Mindreading. Oxford University Press, Oxford (2006)

Gray, H.M., Gray, K., Wegner, D.M.: Dimensions of mind perception. Science **315**(5812), 619 (2007)

Gray, K., Wegner, D.M.: Feeling robots and human zombies: Mind perception and the uncanny valley. Cognition **125**(1), 125–130 (2012)

Hawkins, J., Blakeslee, S.: On Intelligence: How a New Understanding of the Brain Will Lead to the Creation of Truly Intelligent Machines. Henry Holt, New York (2004)

Hofstadter, D.R.: Gödel, Escher, Bach: An Eternal Golden Braid. Basic Books, New York (1979)

Hurley, S.: Understanding simulation. Res. **77**(3), 755–774 (2008)

Kane, R.: The Significance of Free Will. Oxford University Press, Oxford (1998)

Kaptelinin, V., Nardi, B.: Affordances in HCI: toward a mediated action perspective. Paper Presented at the SIGCHI Conference on Human Factors in Computing Systems (2012)

Keijsers, M.: Robot bullying. Doctoral dissertation, University of Canterbury. Research repository of University of Canterbury (2020). https://ir.canterbury.ac.nz/handle/10092/100776

Kieras, D.E.: A summary of the EPIC cognitive architecture. In: Chipman, S.E.F. (ed.) The Oxford Handbook of Cognitive Science, pp. 27–48. Oxford University Press, Oxford (2017)

Kim, J.: Causation, nomic subsumption, and the concept of event. J. Philos. **70**(8), 217–236 (1973)

Kissel, A.: Free will, the self, and video game actions. Ethics Inf. Technol. **23**(3), 177–183 (2020). https://doi.org/10.1007/s10676-020-09542-2

Knobe, J., Nichols, S.: Free will and the bounds of the self. In: Kane, R. (ed.) The Oxford Handbook of Free Will, 2nd edn., pp. 530–554. Oxford University Press, New York (2011)

Kotseruba, I., Tsotsos, J.K.: 40 years of cognitive architectures: Core cognitive abilities and practical applications. Artif. Intell. Rev. **53**(1), 17–94 (2020)

Laird, J.E., Newell, A., Rosenbloom, P.S.: SOAR: an architecture for general intelligence. Artif. Intell. **33**(1), 1–64 (1987)

Li, X., Hammer, P., Wang, P., Xie, H.: Functionalist emotion model in NARS. In: Iklé, M., Franz, A., Rzepka, R., Goertzel, B. (eds.) AGI 2018. LNCS (LNAI), vol. 10999, pp. 119–129. Springer, Cham (2018). https://doi.org/10.1007/978-3-319-97676-1_12

Markram, H., et al.: Reconstruction and simulation of neocortical microcircuitry. Cell **163**(2), 456–492 (2015)

Mori, M.: Bukimi: no tani [the uncanny valley]. Energy **7**(4), 33–35 (1970)

Mori, M., MacDorman, K.F., Kageki, N.: The uncanny valley [from the field]. IEEE Robot. Autom. Mag. **19**(2), 98–100 (2012)

Newell, A.: Unified Theories of Cognition. Harvard University Press, Cambridge (1994)

Norman, D.A.: The Psychology of Everyday Things. Basic Books, New York (1988)

O'Connor, T.: Why agent causation? Philos. Top. **24**(2), 143–158 (1996)

Rifkin, J.: The Empathic Civilization: The Race to Global Consciousness in a World in Crisis. Penguin, New York (2009)

Seibt, J., Nørskov, M., Hakli, R. (eds.): Sociable Robots and the Future of Social Relations: Proceedings of Robo-Philosophy 2014, vol. 273. IOS Press, Amsterdam (2014)

Strawson, P.F.: Freedom and Resentment and Other Essays. Routledge, London (2014)

Tegmark, M.: Life 3.0: Being Human in the Age of Artificial Intelligence. Knopf, New York (2017)

Trope, Y., Liberman, N.: Construal-level theory of psychological distance. Psychol. Rev. **117**(2), 440–463 (2010)

Turing, A.: Computing machinery and intelligence. Mind **59**(1950), 433–460 (1950)

Vallverdú, J., Trovato, G.: Emotional affordances for human–robot interaction. Adapt. Behav. **24**(5), 320–334 (2016)

Waytz, A., Gray, K., Epley, N., Wegner, D.M.: Causes and consequences of mind perception. Trends Cogn. Sci. **14**(8), 383–388 (2010)

Wang, S., Lilienfeld, S., Rochat, P.: The uncanny valley: existence and explanations. Rev. Gen. Psychol. **19**(4), 393–407 (2015)

Weizenbaum, J.: ELIZA—a computer program for the study of natural language communication between man and machine. Commun. ACM **9**(1), 36–45 (1966)

Sensor Sharing Marketplace

Dimitrios Georgakopoulos[✉] and Anas Dawod

Swinburne University of Technology, Melbourne, VIC 3122, Australia
{dgeprgakopoulos,adawod}@swin.edu.au

Abstract. The Internet of Things (IoT) incorporates billions of Internet-connected sensors, and the number of such IoT devices is currently growing rapidly. The proposed Sensor Sharing Marketplace (SenShaMart) permits IoT applications to find IoT sensors that are owned and managed by other parties in IoT (which we refer to as IoT sensor providers), integrate them, and pay for using their data. SenShaMart benefits include IoT senor reuse, increase of new sensor deployment by providing a revenue generation scheme for IoT sensor providers, and cost reduction for IoT application development by eliminating the need to procure and deploy their own sensors. SenShaMart incorporates a specialized blockchain that stores all information needed to describe, query, integrate, pay for, and use IoT sensors and their data. IoT applications interact with SenShaMart via a suite of services that access and manage the sensor and transaction information that is stored in the SenShaMart blockchain. This paper presents the SenShaMart architecture. It describes SenShaMart's specialized blockchain and related services. The paper also presents remaining research problems and directions for fully realizing SenShaMart.

Keywords: Internet of Things · Blockchain · IoT sensor marketplace · IoT sensor sharing

1 Introduction

The Internet of Things (IoT) is the latest Internet evolution that incorporates billions of IoT devices that include sensors, RFIDs, wearables, power meters, vehicles, and industrial machines [1]. Such IoT devices (which we also refer to as IoT sensors or simply sensors) incorporate microprocessors, and communication modules that enable them to connect to the internet, exchange data, and provide information to IoT applications and their users [2]. Major industry players estimate that the number of IoT sensors in 2030 will reach anywhere from twenty-five billion to 125 billion [3] and they will be generating 79.4 zettabytes (ZB) of data [4]. Due to its unprecedented ability to observe the physical world and to provide high-value information, IoT can address many grand challenges in our society that were extremely hard to solve before due to lack of timely and accurate information. However, the following main challenges remain: 1) IoT applications currently include the procurement, deployment, and maintenance of all the IoT sensors that they need, and 2) the cost of procuring, deploying, and maintaining the required IoT sensors often exceeds the short-term benefits of many IoT applications.

M. Luo and L.-J. Zhang (Eds.): EDGE 2022, LNCS 13732, pp. 64–79, 2022.
https://doi.org/10.1007/978-3-031-23470-5_6

In addition, IoT applications that can improve response to rapid-onset disasters, such as bush fires, cyclones, floods, tsunamis, or even COVID-19 hotspots and outbreaks, are currently impossible due to the short timeframe available to deploy the substantial number of sensors that are needed for timely detection of these. Therefore, efficient sharing of existing IoT sensors and related costs among IoT applications is critical in achieving both a positive benefit/cost ratio and enabling response to rapid-onset events. For example, the negative impact of climate change in agriculture can be mitigated by 1) using IoT sensors that provide the information needed to determine how various plants perform under changing environmental conditions across Australia and the world [6], and 2) planting crops consisting of species of plants that tolerate best the challenging conditions (e.g., increased drought, annual solar radiation, soil deterioration, locust, etc.) at each region or farm. However, the procurement, deployment, and maintenance of IoT sensors that are needed to monitor micro-climate, soil humidity, solar radiation and crop performance are difficult to scale up and incredibly expensive. An alternative solution is to use existing IoT sensors that have been deployed by farmers and agribusinesses for their own purposes to collect the data needed for climate change mitigation, as this minimizes the effort, cost, and timeframe for responding to the effects of climate change.

Sharing and reusing existing IoT sensors is currently severely hindered by lack of a comprehensive solution that permits IoT sensor application (which we refer to as client applications or simply sensor clients) to discover existing sensors provided by other parties (which we refer to as IoT sensor provider applications or simply sensor providers), (re)use them to harvest data they need, and to pay their provider(s) for this. Related research for IoT sensor discovery that involves formulating and executing queries on sensor descriptions supplied by their providers, suffers from severe limitations in achieving both the sensor description and query tasks. Specific challenges in sensor description include: (1) a rapidly expanding volume and variety of IoT sensors that are often owned/controlled by different people and organizations, and (2) both insufficient standards and in addition limited use of such standards in describing existing sensors. For example, leading standards for semantic description of sensors and their data, such as SSN [7] and SOSA [8], do not support sensor identification and mobile sensors. Furthermore, these standards are not widely used because semantic sensor description requires both significant effort and considerable expertise in RDF-based ontology definition/use. Even assuming that all available sensors are described adequately, the following challenges in querying semantic sensor descriptions must be addressed: (1) Semantic query languages, such as SPARQL, are complex and hard to use for querying the descriptions of available sensors (for similar reasons that sematic RDF ontologies are complex and hard to use for sensor description); (2) The scalability of computing SPARQL queries is currently limited and a more efficient solution is needed to compute global sensor query results across IoT; and (3) IoT sensors are volatile, so tracking sensor availability information as existing IoT sensors are taken off and new ones introduced is an open research problem. Finally, IoT client applications must have an unfettered right to discover any sensor offered by any IoT sensor provider. This can only be ensured by a trusted sensor discovery solution that guarantees that no organization or individual can ever prevent or even monopolize access to any available IoT sensor.

Another major challenge in achieving sensor sharing/reuse and promoting the deployment of more sensors in IoT is supporting cost-sharing between the sensor providers and sensor clients via a pay-as-you-go model. This must include payment and compensation transactions that permit any IoT sensor client application to dynamically select, pay, and use any collection of sensors it needs even when multiple sensor providers provide sensors. If any sensor(s) required by an IoT application cannot be found or is unavailable and no alternative sensor(s) are available, the entire transaction must be aborted and result in no payment and no use of any other selected sensor. If a payment is successfully completed, transactional support for compensation is required to reverse payment when any specific sensor stops providing data as agreed by its provider. While transaction models and mechanisms have been thoroughly researched, the main challenge here is to develop a transaction model and mechanism that is not owned or controlled by any client, provider or other third party, as trust is a fundamental requirement for sensor discovery, payment and use across the entire IoT ecosystem.

To address these considerable challenges, novel contributions of this paper include a trusted IoT *Sensor Sharing Marketplace*, which we refer to as *SenShaMart*. SenShaMart provides IoT *Registration, Query, Integration* and *Payment* services for IoT sensors that are provided and used by different parties. IoT clients interact with SenShaMart to discover, integrate, pay for, and use IoT sensors that have been registered in SenShaMart by their providers. To support this, SenShaMart manages all information needed for such transactions in a distributed ledger, we refer to as *SenShaMart blockchain (SB)*. SB is specifically designed for managing 1) IoT sensor description and integration information that are needed to discover, select, and communicate with sensors that are made available by IoT sensor provider applications, and 2) payment transaction records between sensor clients and providers that may include multiple dynamically selected IoT sensors per client and corresponding payments to different sensor providers. SenShaMart supports payment records that ensure the atomicity, consistency, isolation, and durability (ACID) of transactions across SB by guaranteeing that IoT sensor client applications either get and pay for all the sensors they need, or nothing happens. In addition, SenShaMart also supports compensating re-imbursement transactions whenever any sensor(s) stop delivering the data to an IoT sensor client that has already paid for this. This allows IoT sensor clients to make dynamic decisions in finding, using, and paying for sensor provider by multiple providers.

Unlike other existing blockchain-based solutions that store the IoT sensor data in the blockchain (which can make the blockchain a bottleneck and significantly reduce the scalability of such solutions) [16], SB only stores IoT sensor metadata. Therefore, SB provides excellent scalability that is achieved by eliminating all blockchain transactions that are generated by storing and retrieving IoT sensor data observations.

Several sensor description schemas and ontologies have been developed for IoT sensors, including Sensor Web Enablement [9], the Semantic Core Ontology [8], the Semantic Sensor Network (SSN) ontology [7], SOSA [8] and OGC/W3C [11] standard. These provide machine-readable descriptions of IoT sensors that permit IoT applications to query and manually integrate IoT sensors. However, as noted earlier semantic descriptions of IoT sensors are currently rare due to the effort and expertise required to develop them and even when they are available do not provide information required to support IoT sensor identification, mobility, automatic integration, and payment. In this project we intend to extend the SOSA standard [8] by including sensor ID, location, integration endpoint, integration protocol, provider, cost, and data contract. Further, this project will develop a suite of machine learning-based techniques that will analyze IoT data streams from sensors that have no available/provided SOSA or SSN-based descriptions and will automatically generate corresponding sensor metadata that are compatible with the extended SOSA-based ontology and can be automatically inserted in the SB via SenShaMart's Registration service. To accomplish that we are building on our existing research outcomes on sensor data stream classification [12, 34] to devise novel machine learning models for extending SOSA ontologies with new concepts that are derived from sensor data stream classification. Automatic classification of sensors remains a major challenge due to the variety and heterogeneity of IoT sensors and their data. For example, [33] proposed to annotate IoT sensor data with the SSN ontology-based description, and [35] proposed a rule-based reasoning approach to complement this information for supporting sensor integration. However, all existing solutions to date require highly accurate descriptions/metadata of IoT sensors that are often unavailable, and even with that being available the semantic metadata-based approaches that have been proposed do not fully support sensor discovery, integration, and payment.

General purpose semantic query languages, such as SPARQL, can be used to query SOSA-based IoT sensor descriptions and other metadata. For example, Chun et al. [14] proposed a SPARQL-based sensor query solution, but this work did not propose any specific ontology for sensor description. Further to that, the authors have successfully used SPARQL to query SSN-based IoT sensor descriptions in OpenIoT [15]. However, SPARQL query descriptions are too complex for non-technical sensor providers. More importantly, SPARQL query processing over a distributed ledger, such as SB, is slow and inefficient because it requires the retrieval of sensor metadata from the ledger, their conversion to triples, and the insertion the resulting triples into a triple store before the actual SPARQL can be processed. This will not scale up to support the billions of sensors in IoT. To realize SenShaMart we envision 1) devising an easy-to-use sensor query language that will provide the constructs needed to query the properties of available sensors and their data observations, as well as the sensor location, cost, and data contract, 2) incorporating a triple store in the SB nodes, and 3) developing novel blockchain-based indexing techniques that provide fast access to semantically clustered sensor metadata stored in the SB. For sensor integration, we expect that each provider will specify a standard integration protocol and an endpoint link for each sensor they provide and include these in the SB ledger during the sensor registration. IoT applications that select specific sensors are then responsible for retrieving their endpoints and protocols from the SB and use it to integrate them. Sensor integration is not a major research challenge because most existing IoT platforms support several standard protocols (e.g., MQTT) for automatically integrating IoT sensors. Therefore, any IoT client application that uses an IoT platform can automatically integrate any sensor by simply proving its endpoint and protocol to the IoT platform.

Finally, in realizing SenShaMart will also devise a novel pay-as-you-go transaction model and a corresponding cross-blockchain mechanism for supporting trustworthy transactions between IoT sensor clients and providers that involve sensor selection, payment, activation of sensor data flow, and payment compensation when any sensors stop providing data observation as specified in its data contract. The challenge here is that an IoT client application may require data from multiple sensors to achieve its aim, and we must prevent situations where 1) any application pays for and activates the data flow(s) of some of the needed sensors before finding that other sensors have become unavailable since the time the application completed its sensor query and selected the sensors it needs, and 2) after the sensor payment is completed, e.g., a sensors stop providing data or its provider violates another related aspect in its data contract with an IoT application. To prevent this from happening, SenShaMart requires a novel blockchain transaction management mechanism across sensor selection, sensor payment, sensor data flow activation, and payment compensation that manages all relevant information distributed in different blocks of the SB leger.

The remainder of this paper is organized as follows: Sect. 2 presents the proposed architecture of SenShaMart. Section 3 describes the SenShaMart blockchain, while Sect. 4 describes the SenShaMart services. Section 5 describes further research and concludes the paper.

2 Trusted IoT Sensor Sharing Market (SenShaMart)

As illustrated in Fig. 1, the SenShaMart is comprised of a collection of distributed nodes. SenShaMart nodes interact via the SenShaMart Blockchain (SB) that has been specifically designed to store and manage all information needed for IoT sensors description, query, integration, and payment, which we collectively refer to as IoT sensor metadata.

Figure 2 illustrates the architecture of the individual SenShaMart nodes in Fig. 1. As shown in Fig. 2, each SenShaMart node includes the following:

- A SB node, which is responsible for blockchain-related functions including maintaining a ledger of all IoT sensor metadata, verifying generated blocks, and contributing to SenShaMart consensus. The SB is discussed further in Sect. 3.
- IoT sensor registration, IoT sensor query, IoT sensor payment, and IoT sensor integration services, which allow IoT sensor client applications to query IoT sensors controlled and maintained by other parties (which we refer to as IoT sensor providers), integrate such IoT sensors and their data observations, and pay for these. IoT sensor integration service is compressed to IoT sensor access control service and IoT sensor data forwarding service. The IoT sensor data forwarding service, which manages the flow of IoT sensor data from the IoT sensors to the IoT sensor client applications, is autonomically controlled by the IoT sensor access control service. All SenShaMart services use the SB to manage and distribute the IoT sensor metadata (which, as we noted earlier, are used exclusively for IoT sensor description, query, integration, and payment) across all SenShaMart nodes. The SenShaMart services are discussed further in Sect. 4.

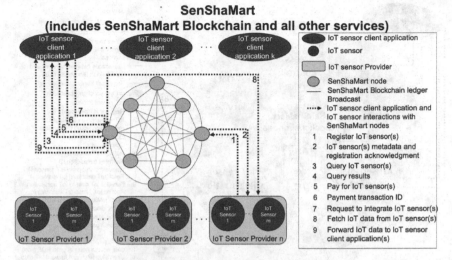

Fig. 1. High-level architecture of SenShaMart.

IoT sensor client applications and IoT sensor providers can interact with SenShaMart via the services in any of its nodes. For example, as illustrated in Fig. 1, an IoT Sensor Provider may register its IoT sensors via a specific SenShaMart node but forward IoT sensor data via another node. Similarly, an IoT sensor client application may query, pay, and integrate IoT sensors via services in different SenShaMart nodes.

To maintain compatibility with existing protocols that currently allow IoT sensor client applications to interact with IoT sensors and obtain their data observations, Sen-ShaMart (and more specifically, its IoT Data Forwarding service) supports many standard communications protocols that are commonly available in most existing IoT platforms. Without a loss of generality, in this paper, we assume that the IoT Data Forwarding service utilizes the standard MQTT protocol [18] that is supported by virtually all existing IoT platforms. Other widely supported communication protocols like CoAP [19] are similarly supported, but they are outside of the scope of this paper.

3   SenShaMart Blockchain

This is a blockchain designed and implemented specifically for storing the IoT sensor metadata that are needed for IoT sensors description, query, integration, and payment. In this section, we explain how SenShaMart manages the metadata needed for its novel IoT sensor payment, integration, and access control functionalities, which are being introduced by this paper. In Sects. 3.1 and 3.2, we present the SB nodes and SB support for semantic description and query of IoT sensors and their data, and the SB support for integrating and paying IoT sensors.

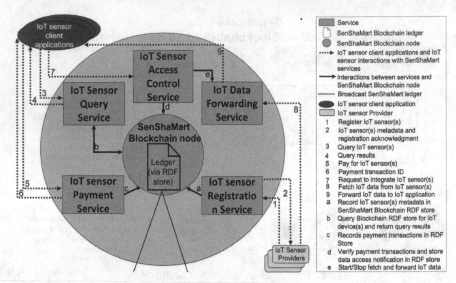

Fig. 2. SenShaMart node architecture

3.1 SenShaMart Blockchain Nodes

The SB is public, and any node can join it the same way as adding a new node to Bitcoin [20] or many other similar public blockchains. Similarly, SB nodes are responsible for generating new blocks, contributing to SB consensus, and verifying newly generated blocks across the entire SB.

Unlike other existing blockchains (e.g., Bitcoin [20]), SB nodes provide the following novel features that support IoT sensor discovery, integration, and payment:

- A copy of the SB ledger that contains all IoT sensor metadata. This is a semantic ledger that records the SSN-based descriptions of IoT sensors and their data, as well as other metadata used for IoT sensor integration, payment, and access control.
- An RDF triple store that is used to store the above IoT sensor metadata records as triples organized in blocks, which we refer to as SenShaMart ledger blocks, or just SenShaMart blocks. SenShaMart's RDF triple store provides highly efficient on-blockchain processing of semantic queries involving IoT sensor metadata.
- An interface that allows only the SenShaMart services to access SenShaMart blocks in the SB.

When a new SenShaMart block is created in a node, this SB node broadcasts newly generated SenShaMart block to all other SB nodes to make the SenShaMart ledger consistent across all SB nodes. The broadcast mechanism is like other existing blockchains (e.g., Bitcoin [20]). IoT sensor description and query are discussed further next, in Sect. 3.2.

3.2   SenShaMart Blockchain Support for IoT Sensor Description, Query, Integration, and Payment

The SB is specifically designed to support semantic IoT sensor query, integration, and payment. To support IoT sensor query, the IoT Sensor Providers record semantic descriptions of their IoT sensors and their data in the SenShaMart ledger via the IoT Sensor Registration Service (which is discussed further in Sect. 4.1). IoT sensor descriptions are based on our SenShaMart ontology. The SenShaMart Ontology provides a common vocabulary that allows IoT sensor provider and clients to describe, query, integrate, and pay IoT sensors. To serve this purpose, the SenShaMart ontology addresses the main short comings of the SSN/SOSA ontologies [7, 8] when these are applied to IoT sensor discovery. The SSN/SOSA extensions included in the SenShaMart Ontology are:

- *Sensor ownership*: We proposed using a Public Key (PK) as identifier for each IoT sensor provider and using this PK as ownership for all providers of IoT sensors. PK offers a unique and anonymous identifier for providers. IoT sensors might have a multi-level ownership such an IoT sensor is owned by a department in organization and managed by two persons. Therefore, the ownership concept includes multiple attributes, which are Organization, Department, and Person that allows a shared or multi-level ownership. Each one of these attributes can include one or multiple PKs to insure providing ownership for different scenarios.
- *Sensor Geospatial Location*: this concept provides the necessary geospatial information to specify the location of IoT sensors. This concept includes three attributes which are latitude, longitude, and elevation. The latitude and longitude attributes provide the information about the IoT sensor location in two dimensions; the elevation attribute provides further information about the height of the IoT sensor. The geospatial location information is important for querying IoT sensors. IoT applications may choose to query IoT sensors in specific country, city, or area; in this case latitude and longitude information helps filter IoT sensors based on the IoT application needs. The elevation information is important to understand the functionality of the IoT sensor. For example, the elevation information can differentiate two thermometers, one deployed on the street and the other deployed on top of a skyscraper. This information helps IoT sensor client applications to query specific IoT sensors for their needs.
- *Sensor Integration:* this concept describes all needed information for helping SenShaMart to integrate IoT sensors. The integration concept includes several attributes to address different protocols/techniques for integrating IoT sensors. These attributes are Protocol, Unified Resource Identifier (URI), Topic, Token, Address, and Endpoint. The protocol attribute gives information about the internet protocol used to integrate the IoT sensor such as MQTT [18]; this attribute is important for IoT sensor integration service to establish the communication channel based on this protocol. Endpoint attribute represents an address or URL that allows IoT sensor integration service to communicate with the IoT sensor; this attribute is usually used with CoAP [19]. A URI attribute represents an address or URL that allows IoT sensor integration service to communicate with the IoT service; this attribute is usually used to identify MQTT broker. Address attribute represents an address or URL that allows IoT sensor integration service to communicate with the IoT sensor; this attribute is used for any other

protocol or technique. Topic attribute can be used specifically for MQTT protocol to allow communication between IoT sensor integration service and the IoT sensor. Token attribute represents a key to activate IoT data flow.

- *Cost of Using IoT Sensors*: this concept provides necessary information for describing the cost of using IoT sensors. This concept includes two attributes to describe the cost of using IoT sensors, which are cost per unit of time (e.g., minute), and cost per unit of amount of IoT data (e.g., Kbyte). IoT sensor provider may choose one of these attributes or both to calculate the required payment for using the IoT sensor.

- *Sensor Unique Identification (ID)*: this concept provides all required identities that are used to identify, integrate, and pay IoT sensors. This concept includes several attributes including Sensors ID, Sensor name, TimeStamp, and Pay IDs. Also, it includes a string that matches the description of the IoT sensor or the provider to give better understanding about the IoT sensor, which is called Sensor name. Sensors ID attribute includes unique identification for each IoT sensor to differentiate two identical IoT sensors. TimeStamp attribute includes the time of creating the IoT sensor metadata to keep track of any update for the IoT sensor in the future. Pay IDs attribute includes unique identifications used to allow IoT applications to pay for using the IoT sensor. Each IoT sensor may have more than one Pay ID to support different payment techniques such as PayPal and cryptocurrencies like Bitcoin.

As noted earlier in Sect. 3.1, SenShaMart nodes incorporate triple stores that store such IoT sensor metadata triplets in the local copy of the blocks that comprise the SB ledger. This solution allows the IoT sensor query service (which is discussed further in Sect. 4.2) to efficiently process SPARQL [21] IoT sensor-related queries that enable IoT sensor client applications to find the IoT sensors they need.

To allow IoT sensor client applications to automatically integrate and pay for the IoT sensors they use, we extend our SenShaMart ontology to include unified measurement templates, IoT sensor payment transactions, and IoT data access notifications. More specifically, a unified measurement template allows an IoT Sensor Provider to describe a specific IoT sensor and its data using concepts from the SenShaMart ontology. This unified measurement template is subsequently used by all IoT sensor client applications that use these IoT sensors to integrate the IoT sensor and its data observations. All unified templates use concepts from/are consistent with the SenShaMart ontology.

To support IoT sensor payment, we propose adding a novel IoT sensor payment transaction concept in the SenShaMart ontology and recording payment transaction logs based on this concept in the SenShaMart ledger. These permit SenShaMart to manage IoT sensor payments via the SB. To maintain access to the IoT sensor data while the payment lasts, we have introduced the concept of IoT data access notification in the SenShaMart Ontology and SenShaMart records related access notification instances in the SenShaMart ledger. To support IoT sensor query, integration, payment transactions and related data access, the SB blocks include public and encrypted sections. The public block section includes semantics description of the IoT sensors and their data observations, IoT Sensor IDs, and Provider's IDs. The encrypted block section includes the information in the IoT sensor integration concept. The public section is used for discovering (i.e., describing and querying) IoT sensors, while the encrypted part is used for integrating, paying, and controlling access to IoT sensors and their data. For example,

the IoT sensor token/topic and endpoint are encrypted to prevent IoT sensor client applications from integrating and using IoT sensors without a permission from SenShaMart
(which is only granted after payment is received and while payment lasts). Only specific services in the SenShaMart nodes can decrypt such encrypted information. The
SenShaMart services are presented next in Sect. 4.

4   SenShaMart Services

This section presents the SenShaMart services that are the only components of the
SenShaMart nodes that can access the SB.

4.1   IoT Sensor Registration Service

This service allows IoT sensor providers to register their IoT sensors in SenShaMart
to make them discoverable (via SPARQL queries) by IoT sensor client applications.
As illustrated in Fig. 2, the IoT Sensor Providers interact directly with the IoT sensor
registration service to provide their IoT sensor metadata and their information that is
needed for payment transactions (as discussed in Sect. 4.3). Each provider can register
multiple IoT sensors together. Next, the IoT sensor registration service generates the
metadata for the registered IoT sensor(s), sends it to the IoT sensor provider, and submits
it to SB by inserting this in a block that needs to be verified by the SB nodes. When the
block verification is complete, the IoT sensor metadata is stored in the SB ledger via the
RDF triple store and can be queried via any SenShaMart node. To create the IoT sensor
metadata, the IoT sensor registration service (1) uses the SenShaMart Ontology (which
was presented in Sect. 3.2 to generate publicly accessible metadata for all IoT sensors
being registered and (2) encrypt sensitive IoT sensor metadata, such as the IoT sensor
token and end point. Once IoT sensor metadata of all IoT sensors being registered are
stored successfully in SB, the IoT sensor registration service sends an acknowledgment
to the IoT sensor provider. The IoT sensor registration service is also responsible for
updating the IoT sensor description by creating a new IoT sensor metadata linking the
IoT sensor ID of the earlier one. Note that in this case, both IoT sensor metadata versions
will be visible on SB as the information stored inside SB is immutable (as in all other
existing blockchains).

4.2   IoT Sensor Query Service

This service supports querying the IoT sensor metadata that are stored in SenShaMart
ledger by using one or more search conditions that are provided by each IoT sensor client
application. Search conditions may involve IoT sensor attributes (e.g., the sensor type,
location, cost, provider), the sensors that are incorporated in the IoT sensors (e.g., sensor
type, accuracy, range), and the data observations they produce (e.g., solar radiation,
pressure, temperature). The IoT sensor query service converts the submitted search
conditions to a corresponding SPARQL query and processes this query efficiently using
the built-in triple store in its SenShaMart node. For example, to find all IoT sensors
that have a temperature sensor with range greater than 100 degrees, an IoT sensor client

application submits the following search conditions as value name pairs that include concepts from the SenShaMart ontology: (Sensor) Type: Temperature, Range: >100. SPARQL query generation is based on the following principles:

- A SPARQL query contains two essential clauses, which are PREFIX and SELECT, and several elective clauses such as WHERE and FILTETR. The PREFIX clause defines the ontology that will be used in the query. By default, the PREFIX in our query-generating function is SenShaMart ontology.
- The SELECT clause is responsible for determining the structure of the query response. In this query example, the query structure consists of the "Type" and "Range" concepts.
- The WHERE clause is responsible for providing the graph pattern to match against the data graph, which is provided in the search conditions. The graph patterns in this query example are "Type" and "Range". "Temperature" and ">100" are represented in the corresponding data graph.
- The FILTER clause contains Boolean expressions to filter the query results to match with the IoT sensor client application needs. In the query example, the filtration is applied on the range of temperature, which should be over one hundred degrees.

For this IoT sensor query example, the IoT sensor query service generates the SPARQL query, as shown in Fig. 3.

```
PREFIX ssn: <https://www.w3.org/ns/ssn/>
SELECT ?type ?range
WHERE {
?IoT_device a type:temperature;
?range
}
FILTER (?range > 100)
```

Fig. 3. SPARQL query generated by IoT sensor query sub-service to support automatic discovery of IoT sensors.

When the query is executed, IoT sensor query service returns a list of IoT sensors that meet the IoT sensor search conditions and all public IoT sensor metadata that are available for each of these IoT sensors. For this IoT sensor query example, the IoT sensor query service generates the SPARQL query, as shown in Fig. 3. When the query is executed, IoT sensor query service returns a list of IoT sensors that meet the IoT sensor search conditions and all public IoT sensor metadata that are available for each of these IoT sensors. The IoT sensor query service also accepts direct SPARQL queries that are formulated using the SenShaMart ontology. While direct (i.e., non-generated by the query service) SPARQL queries allow the use of the full expressive power of SPARQL that may be useful for some IoT sensor client applications, SPARQL queries are hard to formulate and may require expertise that may be beyond the skills of some IoT sensor client application developers [22, 36].

4.3 IoT Sensor Payment Sensor

SenShaMart provides a novel pay-as-you-go mechanism that rewards IoT sensor providers with payments for sharing their IoT sensors. This helps to increase the number of shared IoT sensors that are available for IoT sensor client applications.

To enable IoT sensor payment, IoT sensor providers specify the IoT sensor cost per unit of time (e.g., per minute or Pminutes) or unit of data (e.g., per Kbyte or Pkbyte), as well as the method for receiving payment (e.g., PayPal, Bitcoin, bank transfer), when they register their IoT sensors in SenShaMart via the IoT sensor registration service, which was discussed in Sect. 4.1.

IoT sensor client applications use the IoT sensor payment service to pay for the IoT sensors they select from the query results they obtain from the IoT sensor query service, which was presented in Sect. 4.2. The IoT sensor payment service computes the total payment Ptotal for using IoT sensors by considering: (1) the cost of using IoT sensors per minute Pminutes, multiplied by the number of minutes Nminutes, and (2) the cost of IoT data per Kbyte Pkbyte multiplied by the number of delivered Kbytes Nkbytes, as represented by:

$$P_{total} = P_{Kbyte} * N_{Kbyte} + P_{minutes} * N_{minutes} \qquad (1)$$

As soon as the IoT sensor client application/payer makes the IoT sensor payment, the IoT sensor payment service verifies the payment and creates an IoT sensor payment transaction, as discussed in Sect. 4.3. To perform the latter, the IoT sensor payment service first generates an IoT sensor payment transaction ID and a transaction timestamp. Next, the IoT sensor payment service records these and the selected IoT sensor(s)/provider details in an IoT sensor payment transaction, and submits the transaction to the SB. Each IoT sensor payment transaction can include payments for multiple IoT sensors that are supported by the different providers. The IoT sensor payment transactions are then used by IoT sensor access control service (which is discussed further in Sect. 4.4) to provide access permission to the appropriate IoT client application that has paid for the sensors.

If an IoT sensor client application has not paid for an IoT sensor, the IoT sensor access control service rejects IoT sensor integration requests (i.e., withholds the IoT sensor integration concept) from the application. The IoT sensor client application can only gain access to the IoT sensor if it uses the IoT sensor payment service to pay for the IoT sensor and the payment service has created a transaction that has been successfully verified and added to the SB ledger. This creates an incentive mechanism for IoT sensor providers that motivates them to share more IoT sensors.

4.4 IoT Sensor Access Control Service

IoT sensor client applications gain access to the IoT sensor(s) they have paid for by sending an integration request to the IoT sensor access control service. Integration requests include the following: the ID of the requesting IoT sensor client application, the IDs of the target IoT sensor(s), the ID of the IoT sensor payment transaction that recorded the payment for these IoT sensor(s), and the metadata of targeted IoT sensors that are recorded in the SB ledger. The IoT sensor access control service verifies the IoT sensor payment transaction by matching the target IoT sensor IDs with the IoT sensor IDs recorded in the IoT sensor payment transaction in the SB ledger. If all target IoT sensor IDs match the IDs in a recorded payment transaction, the payment is verified. The IoT sensor access control service can grant the access of IoT sensor(s) to the IoT application for either a duration of time (i.e., if the IoT sensor client application paid for accessing IoT sensor(s) per unit of time) or data size (i.e., if the IoT sensor client application paid for accessing IoT sensor(s) per unit of data size) based on the information in the payment transaction log, which contains the recorded payment transactions (i.e., part of IoT sensor metadata) inside SB ledger as explained in Sect. 3.2. To illustrate, IoT sensor client application A requests for accessing IoT sensor(s) D and paid for them by payment transaction PT. IoT sensor access control service verifies PT by checking that PT has recorded in the payment transaction log PL and D's ID match the ID(s) recorded in PL, as explained earlier. Once the payment is confirmed, there are two scenarios that the IoT sensor access control service can follow:

- If A paid for accessing D per unit of time, the IoT sensor access control calculates the duration of time T of accessing D. Then, each time D pushes new IoT data, the IoT sensor access control checks if the $current\_time - timestamp\_in\_PT \leq T$ is true; if so, it allows the IoT data flow from D to A. Otherwise, it stops the IoT data flow.
- If A paid for accessing D per unit of data size, the IoT sensor access control calculates the total IoT data size S that should flow from D to A. Then, it maintains IoT data counter C, which initially starts with zero ($C = 0$) and then increments with the size of IoT data ($C = C +$ size of new IoT data) every time D pushes new IoT data. The IoT sensor access control checks if $C \leq S$ is true; if so, it allows the IoT data flow from D to A. Otherwise, it stops IoT data flow.

The IoT sensor access control service calculates T and S by dividing the amount of money paid by A from PT over the cost of accessing D per unit of time or data size from IoT sensor metadata as can be seen from the following formulas:

$$T = \text{Amount of Money paid}/\text{Cost Per Unit of Time} \tag{2}$$

$$T = \text{Amount of Money paid}/\text{Cost Per Unit of Data Size} \tag{3}$$

For example, if the cost of accessing D was 10 cents per hour and A paid 50 cents, that means $T = 5$ h. Additionally, if the cost of accessing D was 2 cents per MB and paid 50 cents, which means $S = 25$ MB.

The IoT sensor access control service allows IoT data flow from D to A by instructing the IoT data forwarding service (Sect. 4.5) to fetch IoT data from D and forward it to A. It also stops the IoT data flow by instructing the IoT data forwarding service to stop fetching IoT data from D and forward it to A. Finally, the IoT sensor access control submits IoT data access notification to SB to record the information of integrating A to D in SB ledger.

4.5   IoT Data Forwarding Service

The IoT data forwarding service is responsible for controlling the flow of IoT data from each specific IoT sensor to its client IoT sensor client applications. When the IoT sensor access control service verifies the payment of IoT sensor client application A for accessing the IoT sensor(s) D, it instructs the IoT data forwarding service used in the encrypted endpoint and other standard IoT sensor communication protocol specific information, such as the Topic for MQTT, so D can access D's data via this protocol, and then encapsulates the received IoT data with unified measurement template retrieved from D's metadata. Next, it forwards the encapsulated measurement data to A for the period the payment last made by A. It continues the IoT data flow from D to A until the IoT sensor access control service (discussed further in Sect. 4.4) stops this.

5   Future Research Directions and Conclusion

To fully realize SenShaMart, the following area requires further research:

Novel machine learning (ML) models are required for automatic classification of IoT sensor data streams and automatically extending SOSA/SSN-based ontologies with new concepts extracted from IoT sensor data streams. The ML-based model development will be based on extending the approach we developed in [12], while ontology extension will draw from [33]. The classification models will enable automatic generation of sematic IoT sensor descriptions by analyzing the data stream IoT sensors produce. This will significantly reduce or eliminate the effort and expertise required by IoT sensor provider to develop description of the IoT sensor they offer for use by IoT applications. The ontology extension model will enhance existing SOSA-based ontologies with new concepts drawn from unclassified aspects of the IoT sensor data streams.

A simplified language for the specification of IoT sensor queries and a highly scalable query mechanism for processing SOSA-based IoT sensor descriptions stored in the SenShaMart ledger. The simplified IoT sensor query language will significantly reduce the complexity (and related specification effort and expertise required) of sematic query languages, such as SPARQL, when they are used to specify IoT sensor queries involving many sparsely interconnected SOSA/SSN-based IoT sensor descriptions. Devising a highly efficient query processing mechanism for information distributed across multiple nodes in the SB is critical for allowing IoT applications to quickly find the IoT sensors they need.

The SenShaMart client blockchain need to be extended to support ACID transactions and a related blockchain-based transaction processing mechanism that will support ACID payment and use (i.e., activation of data streams) of multiple IoT sensors owned and managed by multiple providers. Existing blockchains completely lack support for ACID transactions that involve data stored in different blockchain blocks. This problem becomes more challenging as the number of IoT sensor clients, the number of IoT sensors, and/or the number of IoT sensor providers increase.

To conclude, the proposed SenShaMart marketplace achieves the following: (1) makes IoT application development more efficient and cost-effective via enabling sharing and reusing of existing IoT sensors owned and maintained by different sensor providers, (2) promotes deployment of new IoT sensors supported by a revenue generation scheme for their providers, and (3) reduces or eliminates the need to produce, deploy and maintain the IoT sensors each application needs. To realize SenShaMart this paper proposes a novel specialized blockchain and related services for IoT sensor discovery and payment transactions that are completely trusted (i.e., they are not controlled by any individual or organization) and can scale up to support millions of IoT applications and IoT sensors.

References

1. Georgakopoulos, D., Jayaraman, P.P.: Internet of things: from internet scale sensing to smart services. Computing **98**(10), 1041–1058 (2016). https://doi.org/10.1007/s00607-016-0510-0
2. McEwen, A., Cassimally, H.: Designing the Internet of Things, 1st edn. Wiley, Hoboken (2013)
3. ACS: Australia's IoT Opportunity: Driving Future Growth. http://bit.ly/32rdri9. Accessed 20 Feb 2020
4. Enabling the Internet of Things for Australia, An Industry Report, Communications Alliance Internet of Things Think Tank, June 2015. http://bit.ly/2F4vXBu. Accessed 21 Feb 2020
5. IDC: The growth in connected IoT sensors. https://www.idc.com/getdoc.jsp?containerId=prU S45213219. Accessed June 2020
6. Forbes: How The Internet Of Things Will Help Fight Climate Change. http://bit.ly/37VpGF3. Accessed 21 Feb 2020
7. Compton, M., et al.: The SSN ontology of the W3C semantic sensor network incubator group. J. Web Semant. **17**, 25–32 (2012)
8. Haller, A., et al.: The SOSA/SSN ontology: a joint W3C and OGC standard specifying the semantics of sensors, observations, actuation, and sampling. In: Semantic Web. IOS Press (2018)
9. Jirka, S., Bröring, A., Stasch, C.: Discovery mechanisms for the sensor web. Sensors **9**(4), 2661–2681 (2009)
10. Hunter, J.: Enhancing the semantic interoperability of multimedia through a core ontology. IEEE Trans. Circ. Syst. Video Technol. **13**, 49–58 (2003)
11. Russomanno, D.J., Kothari, C., Thomas, O.: Building a sensor ontology: a practical approach leveraging ISO and OGC models. In: The 2005 International Conference on Artificial Intelligence (IC-AI 2005), pp. 637–643 (2005)
12. Montori, F., Liao, K., Jayaraman, P.P., Bononi, L., Sellis, T., Georgakopoulos, D.: Classification and annotation of open internet of things datastreams. In: Hacid, H., Cellary, W., Wang, H., Paik, H.Y., Zhou, R. (eds.) WISE 2018. LNCS, vol. 11234, pp. 209–224. Springer, Cham (2018). https://doi.org/10.1007/978-3-030-02925-8_15
13. Fortuna, B., Grobelnik, M., Mladenic, D.: OntoGen: semi-automatic ontology editor. In: Smith, M.J., Salvendy, G. (eds.) Human Interface 2007. LNCS, vol. 4558, pp. 309-318. Springer, Heidelberg (2007). https://doi.org/10.1007/978-3-540-73354-6_34
14. Chun, S., Seo, S., Oh, B., Lee, K.-H.: Semantic description, discovery and integration for the internet of things. In: Proceedings of the 2015 IEEE 9th International Conference on Semantic Computing (IEEE ICSC 2015) (2015)
15. Soldatos, J., et al.: OpenIoT: open source internet-of-things in the cloud. In: Podnar Žarko, I., Pripužić, K., Serrano, M. (eds.) Interoperability and Open-Source Solutions for the Internet of Things. LNCS, vol. 9001, pp. 13–25. Springer, Cham (2015). https://doi.org/10.1007/978-3-319-16546-2_3
16. Popov, S.: The tangle, p. 131 (2016)
17. Alphand, O., et al.: IoTChain: a blockchain security architecture for the internet of things. In: 2018 IEEE Wireless Communications and Networking Conference (WCNC), 15–18 April 2018, pp. 1–6 (2018). https://doi.org/10.1109/WCNC.2018.8377385

18. Hunkeler, U., Truong, H.L., Stanford-Clark, A.: MQTT-S—a publish/subscribe protocol for wireless sensor networks. In: 2008 3rd International Conference on Communication Systems Software and Middleware and Workshops (COMSWARE 2008), pp. 791–798. IEEE (2008)
19. Shelby, Z., Hartke, K., Bormann, C.: The constrained application protocol (CoAP). 2070-1721 (2014)
20. Nakamoto, S.: Bitcoin: a peer-to-peer electronic cash system (2008)
21. Harris, S., Seaborne, A., Prud'hommeaux, E.: SPARQL 1.1 query language. W3C recommendation, vol. 21, no. 10 (2013)
22. Perera, C., Jayaraman, P.P., Zaslavsky, A., Georgakopoulos, D., Christen, P.: Sensor discovery and configuration framework for the internet of things paradigm. In: 2014 IEEE World Forum on Internet of Things (WF-IoT), pp. 94–99. IEEE (2014)
23. Fast Elliptic Curve Cryptography in plain javascript. (2014). GitHub. https://github.com/indutny/elliptic
24. Ruben, V.: Lightning fast, asynchronous, streaming RDF for JavaScript. Github (2022). https://github.com/rdfjs/N3.js#readme. Accessed 25 Jan 2022
25. Nair, P.R., Dorai, D.R.: Evaluation of performance and security of proof of work and proof of stake using blockchain, p. 283 (2021)
26. Buterin, V.: A next-generation smart contract and decentralized application platform. White paper (2014)
27. A free, open-source ontology editor and framework for building intelligent systems. Stanford University (2016). https://protege.stanford.edu/
28. Comunica, highly modular and flexible query engine platform for the Web. GitHub (2017). https://github.com/comunica/comunica
29. IoT-Data-Simulator. IBA Group, GitHub (2018). https://github.com/IBA-Group-IT/IoT-data-simulator
30. Gatling. Gatling corp (2012). https://gatling.io/
31. Dawod, A., Georgakopoulos, D., Jayaraman, P.P., Nirmalathas, A.: An IoT-owned service for global IoT Device discovery, integration and (re)use. In: 2020 IEEE International Conference on Service Computing (SCC). IEEE (2020)
32. Dawod, A., Georgakopoulos, D., Jayaraman, P.P., Nirmalathas, A., Parampalli, U.: IoT device integration and payment via an autonomic blockchain-based service for IoT device sharing. Sensors 22(4), 1344 (2022)
33. Calbimonte, J.-P., et al.: Deriving semantic sensor metadata from raw measurements. In: Proceedings of 5th International Workshop on Semantic Sensor Networks SSN2012 (2012)
34. Madithiyagasthenna, D., et al.: A solution for annotating sensor data streams - an industrial use case in building management system. In: Proceedings of 21st IEEE International Conference on Mobile Data Management (MDM) (2020)
35. Wei, W., Barnaghi, P.: Semantic annotation and reasoning for sensor data. In: Barnaghi, P., Moessner, K., Presser, M., Meissner, S. (eds.) EuroSSC 2009. LNCS, vol. 5741, pp. 66–76. Springer, Heidelberg (2009). https://doi.org/10.1007/978-3-642-04471-7_6
36. Perera, C., Zaslavsky, A., Compton, M., Christen, P., Georgakopoulos, D.: Semantic-driven configuration of internet of things middleware. In: 2013 Ninth International Conference on Semantics, Knowledge and Grids, pp. 66–73 (2013). https://doi.org/10.1109/SKG.2013.9

Future Lies with Edge Computing

Min Luo(✉)

Services Society, Cumming, GA 30341, USA
Mluo60@gatech.edu

Abstract. This paper presents a relatively comprehensive survey of recent advances in edge computing, including key drivers and business benefits for typical business use cases. A reference architecture with a supporting service model is proposed that can be used as the starting point for any organization to adopt edge computing. A list of challenges and future work is also assembled for both the academic and industrial research and development.

Keywords: Edge computing · Cloud datacenter · Edge datacenter · Internet of Things (IoT) · Tiered architecture · Distributed systems · Distributed DBMS/SQL · Artificial intelligence · Machine learning · Security · Reliability · Scalability

1 Introduction

The evolution to cloud native network functions and distributed cloud computing has enabled service providers to move beyond traditional connectivity-service models, and the scalability and security of the cloud made it ideal for sharing large datasets and providing backup and recovery in the event of a cyberattack or natural disaster. However, applications running with such infrastructure could rely solely on the cloud for storing and processing data and is dependent on internet connectivity – and therefore subject to its possible unreliability. When the internet slows or becomes unavailable, the entire application could slow down or even fail.

Digital transformation has been enabling enterprises to improve operational efficiency and customer satisfaction, with various internet of things (IoT) devices and platforms delivering functionalities and data essential for digitizing products and services. With IoT, businesses can scale up their operations and boost business efficiency, generate new revenue and expand their digital capabilities to provide better operations and become more productive, protected, and profitable. As predicted by Transforma Insights [1], the number of IoT connected devices in the world will grow from 7.6 billion to 24.1 billion from 2019 to 2030. Even though almost 75% of those connected devices use short range technologies such as WiFi, Bluetooth and 802.15.4 (e.g. Zigbee), 5G promised with continuous improvements on bandwidth and costs. Equipped with 5G, the IOT devices/sensors close to the actions can generate so much data that there will be a need for vast storage capacity everywhere and in all forms – public, private and hybrid, with unmatchable demand for bandwidth. In addition, deep learning can transform those devices into an algorithmic or model-based intelligent data capture mechanisms for further upstream processing and analytics. With such capabilities, it also opens door for gigantic volume of data that needs to be transported and further processed.

As annual data volume is expected to grow around 60%, there will never be enough capacity to carry all those data from sources to traditional core data centers. However, data that is created and processed in centralized data centers will drop from the current 90% to 25% by 2025 [Gartner]. So, what does this imply?

It really calls for a computing paradigm shift, as digital transformation has been pushing organizations distributed and expanded toward the edge with better resource and connectivity management, security protection and enforcement. Many real-world applications require real-time decision making, where the downtime or slow response could turn into disaster. Getting the data center closer to the source, where it is generated and consumed, can help resolve critical challenges of cost, flexibility, bandwidth, latency, congestion and data sovereignty.

The future of computing lies with the Edge, as it can empower businesses with many new possibilities in revolutionizing user experiences, products and services, and operational excellence. Digital transformation compels extending and distributing the digital enterprise to the edge, where customers and employees, and enterprise assets are located, and they all need to be connected digitally. Edge computing is just such a distributed computing paradigm that brings data collection, computation, and storage closer to the sources and the execution resources, and eventually closer to the users and applications that consume it. It is an alternative architecture to cloud computing for applications that require high-speed, low latency and high availability. With a data center on/near the edge, measurements or readings that deviate from their norms could be detected instantly, and management system or human-in-charge can make decisions quickly, even respond in real time. With such an infrastructure, most data will not be shipped to the cloud, as they could be processed in an edge data center, no more waiting on a slow connection or other failed central components for critical analysis. Only aggregated data needs to be sent to the cloud for long-term storage and further processing, saving on bandwidth costs, improved availability, and alleviating the issues with the unreliable internet. Not only operations are more efficient, but safety risks can also be significantly reduced. As an emerging revolutionary technology, it can help businesses to overcome limitations imposed by the traditional cloud-based networks, resolve decisive challenges of cost, flexibility, bandwidth, latency, congestion and data sovereignty across a broad range of applications.

Edge solutions will continue to grow and enable digital transformation in every industry, from "Industry 4.0" in manufacturing to smart cities/homes, and to immersive classrooms or retail stores. Edge solutions have historically been managed by the line of business and start shifting to corporate IT for operations to leverage skill sets and optimize cost. With computing resources distributed and the workload spread across the ecosystem, the enterprise can broadly scale its capabilities and extend the impact into more areas of potential businesses.

Pushing data management capabilities toward edge environments can also bring benefits in the form of greater fault tolerance and autonomy. If edge environments do not require centralized resources, then issues with connectivity or unplanned downtime of those resources will not disrupt processes and businesses. Another big benefit of the edge computing model is robust support for data privacy and security. These considerations are critical for applications that handle sensitive data, such as in healthcare or finance, With edge computing, such sensitive data never has to leave the edge.

A recent survey indicated that the line of business already started to see and enjoy the necessity and benefit of edge use cases []:

- Over 40% of the surveyed population are in the mature stage of adoption on specific edge projects, with each vertical industry as follows:
- 52% of retail and public sector are in the mature stage
- 52% of manufacturing are in the mature stage
- 47% finance are in the mature stage
- 43% healthcare are in the mature stage
- 40% energy and utilities are in the mature stage
- Globally and across industry use cases, loss prevention in retail and video-based quality inspection in manufacturing have the highest rate of mature stage adoption (59%).
- 58% of respondents told us they were adopting 5G and edge technologies to remain competitive.

So edge computing is already here, and the future of the digital transformation lies with the Edge! In this survey, we will first review the architecture and services of edge computing and summarize a list of typical business use cases that enterprises can immediately focus on. We will continue with a proposed reference architecture for edge computing, together with a comprehensive service model. Finally, we present some in-depth discussion on important issues that need to be further addressed, from both business, organization and technology perspectives.

2 Necessity of Edge Computing – Cases from the Real World

As discussed before, organizations are now shifting from a centralized cloud to a decentralized model. Edge computing will be an enabler for a broad range of use cases. Together with 5G, the new ecosystem promotes an open programing model for application developers to create business values. By having more capacity and power, better access to fast and widespread networks (5G, satellite), and smarter machines with AI/ML, many futuristic possibilities become reality. Organizations will become more operationally agile and efficient with better decision making and user experience.

Many edge use cases have been partially or fully implemented across industries and multiple cities using diverse network environments and security controls. Edge computing can be deployed for use cases that require low-latency responses, where large volume of data is created but cannot affordably be sent to a data center, or systems that need to continue operating when their connection goes down. Edge computing can be placed at enterprise premises, inside factory buildings, in homes and vehicles, including trains, planes and private cars. Edge computing can also help protect the climate, improve our health, and alleviate road and city congestions.

Diverse use cases are driving the interest in edge capabilities for data and analytics, from real-time event analytics for system automation, control and maintenance to immersive user experiences that enable autonomous behavior of "things."

2.1 Summary List of Typical Edge Computing Business Use Cases

Table 1 summarized typical business use cases/services and their offered benefits across various industries with different technology enablers.

Business use cases will continue to grow at the edge, including interactions among those "things/devices", other components and services, people at the edge in the entire ecosystem. A typical location, whether a factory, a store, or a home, could have a mix of use cases with a variety of requirements for data collection, processing, analytics, collaborations, and decision making.

3 Fundamentals of Edge Computing – Architecture and Services

The new edge computing architecture should be designed as highly diversified with a distributed model of management, intelligence, and multiple types of networks (from private 5G to multi-cloud to on-premises to public 5G etc.), data centers across multiple environments, together with an increasing number of different types of components, including edge/IoT devices, and a set of well-designed reusable business services. Applications, workloads, and hosting could be placed closer to users and digital assets that are generating or consuming the data, either on-premises or in the cloud. In addition, it should enable software-defined services/microservices development and deployment.

3.1 The Proposed Edge Computing Reference Architecture

Figure 1 is such well-designed tiered architecture for Edge Computing, after an extensive survey of publications on this important topic.

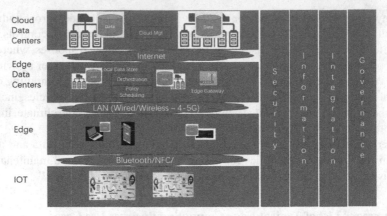

Fig. 1. Tiered reference architecture of edge computing

Such architecture incorporates a holistic ecosystem of infrastructure and management components and services that have been pushed away from the central datacenter (CDC) to the edge data centers (EDC), along with embedded data storage directly on devices where appropriate. Here is a brief review of each layer:

- **IOT (Things) Layer:** Those "things", including mobile phones, wearables and sensors in offices, fields and mines, machinery etc., have just enough bandwidth, memory, processing ability and functionality to collect, sometimes even process, and could execute upon data in real-time autonomously. They are where information is collected, and the eventual analytics-driven decisions and actions are executed. Some devices could be equipped with remote connectivity to other devices and databases at some of the EDCs or even the CDC. Lightweight databases could be placed on some of those devices, for example, on-premises mobile phones or certain advanced sensors.
- **Edge Layer:** This layer hosts devices that have limited (but more powerful than the IOT devices) compute and storage, such as laptops or tablets deployed near mobile base stations, inside shopping malls, branch or local offices or factories. Local datastores are embedded directly to some selected edge mobile and IoT devices, and they largely operate under the databases hosted in EDCs or in other private clouds. Such a layer makes it possible for the ecosystem continue the operation, even with total network failure or breakdown from the cloud DC or other components.
- **Edge Datacenter (EDC) Layer:** This layer bridges the infrastructure between the devices in the Edge Layer and the conventional Cloud Data Center (CDC), such as a public cloud, a collocated provider's cloud, or a private datacenter. EDCs comprise of compute, database server, storage, and applications outside of the CDC, and some gateways that provide the network connectivity back to the CDC. They are normally hosted in multi-sites private or hybrid clouds that are close to where data is generated and consumed, and scaled-down, on-premises edge servers could be easily relocated or fit in. With such additional infrastructure, EDC can significantly improve system operation with reduced latency, bandwidth and operating cost. It also makes the entire system more scalable and reliable, as data could be stored in multiple edge locations,

Table 1. List of representative business use cases

Buziness use cases/servcies	Scenario	Benefits	Key enablers
Immersive/positive customer experiences	AR/VR and mixed reality, computer vision, and artificial intelligence, combined with real and virtual elements of the world for wireless, 3D interactions. It also transports users to a parallel realm to view or explore contents	Enhanced intelligence to create virtual elements and gain 360° coverage of products that enable users explore all its features visually; High product promotion standards for companies aspiring to grow fast; Resources, data, actions/decisions close to the customer on-demand, real-time	AR/VR/MR, vision, AI/ML
Autonomous behavior of "things" (vehicle, machines)	Self-driving vehicles: utilize sensors to gauge location, traffic, environment and safety conditions, make decisions as to how to handle or respond to road conditions or condition changes, and share data with other vehicles; Traffic management: Together with autonomous vehicle data handled by edge d, direct vehicles to paths of least congestion or cicomputingcumvent roadblocks and accidents; Production Line/Machine automation: based on sensed line/machine conditions and discovered manufacturing patterns	Safer operation that take into consideration of vast amounts of data about their surroundings, directions and weather conditions, as well as communicate with other vehicles on the road; Reduced congestion; More efficient digital factories; Predictive maintenance or augmented reality solutions	AR/VR, sensors, vision, AI/ML
Process optimization	With process optimization, time-sensitive rules can be implemented to stream data to the EDC or CDC in batches for immediate analysis and decisions when bandwidth requirement is available. Therefore, the process can be executed at once in real-time and not wait to send a message to the EDC or CDC and then wait again for a response	Able to act in real time; Faster and more resposive process; Automatation	Sensors, data-driven rule-based process automation

(continued)

Table 1. (*continued*)

Buziness use cases/servcies	Scenario	Benefits	Key enablers
Retail	Allows retailers to bring computing power nearer to where data is generated, such as workstations, kiosks, beacons, cameras, point-of-sale systems and sensors; Data from on-premises edge devices can be analyzed in real time and delivered back to store employees as reports and alerts, while other data from multiple sites could be sent to the edge/public cloud for optimizing enterprise predictive models and analytics	Enhance the customer experience; In-store traffic patterns that help retailers better understand their customomersas; Reduced inventory and improved merchandizing	AR/VR, pattern analytics (prediction), real-time data processing
	AR/VR enable potential customers to experience a product or service before they purchase. For seamless digital experiences, frictionless digital interactions, and personalized experiences, data need to be processed close to the VR device. Improve the in-store experience with digital interactions: Grocery and fashion supermarkets help customers easily locate an item by issuing directions with AR. Real-time experience curation: In-store sensors and cameras to identify consumers and then deliver personalized offers as they walk into a store. Immersive VR journeys: VR help customers understand what they are paying for (e.g., the impact of sustainable choices)	AR and VR experiences require rapid processing of data points collected from the edge. For example, a pre-trained machine learning (ML) model can be loaded onto a server deployed at the edge – collecting movement data of a shopper as they stand in front of a screen, the model can deliver inputs to the screen and simulate their movement in a clothing that they intend to purchase. In such use cases, reducing the latency between the source of data and compute resources is the key to building a seamless experience. A latency higher than 20 ms can subtract from the reality of AR and VR experiences and can result in cybersickness	AR/VR, ML/DL

(*continued*)

Table 1. (*continued*)

Buziness use cases/servcies	Scenario	Benefits	Key enablers
Healthcare	High-tech sensors and other medical devices deployed to monitor patients at various locations, while speed of execution or data transfer can be fatal • Emergency calls and response before heart attacks • Vital signs monitoring and response • Non-invasive cancer cell monitoring and response • Smart and personalization health nudges (beyond "get up and move") • Electrolyte imbalance monitoring and notification	By processing real-time data from medical sensors and wearable devices, AI/ML systems are aiding in the early detection of a variety of conditions, such as sepsis and skin cancers; Moving compute power and applications from centralized IT footprints to local edge application servers can reduce latency significantly; Remote monitoring using IoT devices can allow for ongoing visibility into patients' healthcare records - sending alerts to patients and doctors	Sensors, AI/ML, pattern analytics
	Patient monitoring: Monitoring devices (e.g. glucose/blood pressure…) are either not connected, or where they are, large amounts of unprocessed data from devices would need to be stored on a 3rd party cloud with serious security concerns	An edge on the hospital site could process data locally to maintain data privacy. Edge also enables right-time notifications to practitioners of unusual patient trends or behaviours (through analytics/AI), and creation of 360-degree view patient dashboards for full visibility	Sensors, AI/ML, pattern analytics
Smart cities/buildings/home	Internet of Things (IoT) along with AI/ML to quickly identify and remediate problems impacting public safety, citizen satisfaction and environmental sustainability; Enable more effective city traffic management - Optimising bus frequency given fluctuations in demand, managing the opening and closing of extra lanes, and managing autonomous car flows	No need to transport large volumes of traffic data to the central cloud, thus reducing the cost of bandwidth and latency. Benefit to having data hosted on site, both for security and stability considerations	Sensors, AI/ML, pattern analytics
	Smart homes: IoT devices collect and process data from around the house, sending some data to a centralised remote server where it is processed and stored. Problems around backhaul cost, latency, and security	By using edge compute and bringing the processing and storage closer to the smart home, backhaul and roundtrip time is reduced, and sensitive information can be processed at the edge	Sensors, edge data processing (cleaning, aggregation), and limited decision making

(continued)

Table 1. (*continued*)

Buziness use cases/servcies	Scenario	Benefits	Key enablers
Smart manufacturing (factory floor automation)	IoT devices can monitor temperature, humidity, pressure, sound, moisture and radiation to gain insights into service functionality and reduce malfunction risk. It can also be used to prevent catastrophic disasters such as those involving power plants, which might involve damaged assets or risk to human life.; Industrial operations like plant floor processing require a high-speed response with a vast volume of data with the majority of data thrown away, but being able to detect anomalies in the data at the edge enable plant-operators to better detect when to respond to problems on the plant floor. This can lead to higher productivity by avoiding downtime	Reduce malfunction risk for better reliability and safety; Prevent disasters Provide the low-latency required for most process control applications	Sensors, edge data processing (cleaning, aggregation), and limited decision making
	Predictive maintenance: Analyse and detect changes in production lines before a failure occurs	Help bring the processing and storage of data closer to the equipment; Enables IoT sensors to monitor machine health with low latencies and perform analytics in real-time	Sensors, edge data processing (cleaning, aggregation), and limited decision making
Workplace safety	To analyze workspace conditions to ensure safety policies are being followed correctly to protect workers and on-site visitors; Industrial robots can be used with edge computing to reduce risks to human workers and perform routine operations more efficiently by employing actions not subject to fatigue, confusion or misunderstanding	Social distancing intended to reduce risk during the COVID-19 pandemic can be enforced; Industrial robots can replace human workers to perform risky routine operations more efficiently and safely	Sensors, robots
Intelligent farming	Farming in drought-stricken areas can be accomplished with drip-monitoring and measurement systems	With edge computing, network connectivity is no longer a big issue. For example, these systems can make independent decisions that balance ground moisture with available water resources	Sensors, edge data processing (cleaning, aggregation), and limited decision making

(*continued*)

Table 1. (*continued*)

Buziness use cases/servcies	Scenario	Benefits	Key enablers
Energy facility remote monitoring	Oil and gas drilling or transportation failures can be disastrous. All the equipments and pipes, often in remote locations or even dangerous environments (offshore in turbulent weather conditions, underground in mining operations), need to be carefully monitored. Monitoring to ensure critical machinery and systems are protected against disaster or unnecessary wear and tear can increase efficiency and lower costs	Improve both safety and operations. Real-time analytics with processing much closer to the asset, less reliance on good quality connectivity to a centralised cloud	Sensors, edge data processing (cleaning, aggregation), and limited decision making
Mobile big data analytics	AI and analytics are used for fraud detection of financial transactions, for suggesting customer preferences of additional products and services, or for advertising display. These functions require large data stores and analytical processing that use significant storage and CPU resources	Distributing these functions to edge servers can reduce transaction times, resulting in a better customer experience	AI/ML, analytics
Smart grid	Sensors and IoT devices connected to an edge platform in factories, plants and offices are used to monitor energy use and analyze their consumption in real-time	With real-time visibility, enterprises and energy companies can strike new deals, for example where high-powered machinery is run during off-peak times for electricity demand. This can increase the amount of green energy (like wind power) an enterprise consumes	Sensors, edge data processing (cleaning, aggregation), and limited decision making
Video streaming services	Use local network resource knowledge about the environment and available resources to provide more efficient video streaming services; Analyze and push selected content to end-point application servers	Reduce bandwidth requirements and allow users to view higher quality videos	Vedio streaming, edge data processing

(*continued*)

Table 1. (*continued*)

Buziness use cases/servcies	Scenario	Benefits	Key enablers
Metaverse	As the Metaverse becomes prevalent among consumers and businesses, it will need the power of edge computing. Current data centers and networks do not have the speed and capacity to enable an immersive experience! Due to the almost zero latency requirement, metaverse data centers will need to be in very close proximity to the user, and network speeds must be blazing fast. For users all over the world to interact, a fleet of decentralized local edge data centers will be essential	EC is the key for seamless services with Metaverse! puts applications and data as close as possible to users—exactly what's required for a seamless experience, giving users the local computing power necessary while minimizing network-based latency and network-congestion risk	EDC
	All simulated graphical elements must update rapidly in response to the interactions of the participants. The roundtrip latency required to support live, single-participant interactions has to be less than 10 ms, which is much faster than today's latency-sensitive applications, such as video calling and cloud games, that have a roundtrip efficiency of about 100 ms to operate seamlessly	Local storage and processing enable faster response with more immerse experience	EDC

(*continued*)

Table 1. (*continued*)

Buziness use cases/servcies	Scenario	Benefits	Key enablers
Security	With multiple types of networks (from private 5G to multi-cloud to on-premises to public 5G and more) and an increasing number of components, including more IoT/OT devices, need to monitor, manage, protect them all and respond to threats, manage policies, and prioritize vulnerabilities. Audio and video monitoring, biometric scanning and other authorization mechanisms require real time data processing to ensure only the appropriate personnel are allowed in a facility	Rapid response time to address security violations or threats are a key component to successful ongoing business operations	5G, IOT/sensors, AI/ML, vedio surveillance
	AI/ML help augment security at the Edge: Detect and predict the behaviors of malware families, and variations; User Entity Behavior Analytics (UEBA) to detect anomalies in user/entity behavior on the network that augment or supplement to enable faster detection of anomalies; Access management and enforcement control to support risk and trust decision-making related to users and devices trying to access applications, workloads, or other devices; Zero Trust environments to help with continuous, dynamic risk and trust testing based on external security information, security policy, state of the network, identity, the request beings made, and threat intelligence. A "risk/trust" engine can determine the trustworthiness of an entity making a request and feeds that data into a decision engine. The decision engine enforces "grant or deny" based on multiple factors	Enhanced security	AI/ML, behavior analytics, zero-trust

(*continued*)

Table 1. (*continued*)

Buziness use cases/servcies	Scenario	Benefits	Key enablers
	Secure access services edge (SASE) brings together networking and security controls including SD-WAN, CASB (cloud access security broker), SWG (secure web gateway), ZTNA (zero-trust network access), and firewall-as-a-service. Extended detection and response (XDR) against attacks against server/data and user/endpoint devices within the network edge	Integrated security services	SASE
	Video surveillance: Already being deployed at the edge, as well as video analytics. It's a great example of the kinds of data you need to start	Video creates 10 times more data than all other sources combined. Processing them outside of the data center can minimize the amount being moved over the network and stored in DCs. Plus, it allows businesses to make real-time decisions on actionable data	Vedio surveillance
	Dynamic application testing (DAST) and the external attack surface management for vulnerability/risk discovery and prioritization, digital risk protection, BAS (breach and attack simulation), and more. T	Broader view of attack surfaces, including those external-facing software vulnerabilities that could be exploited by threats. For instance, these could be found in shadow IT, assets or applications brought in through M&A, or infrastructure that has been deployed in the cloud without sanctions of the IT department	DAST, BAS
	Consumer Data Privacy: Cloud computing could be dangerous for high sensitivity data (personal, medical, financial etc.) due to the high cost of breaches	More options for "local" security and control at reduced costs	
Cloud gaming	A live feed of the game directly to devices is highly dependent on latency, while the game itself is processed and hosted in data centres	Edge servers close to gamers will reduce latency and provide a fully responsive and immersive gaming experience	EDC

(*continued*)

Table 1. (*continued*)

Buziness use cases/servcies	Scenario	Benefits	Key enablers
Content delivery networks (CDNs)	Early adopters of edge computing, and they continue to grow in many dimensions – quantity, coverage and breadth of services	Caching contents (music, video stream, web pages) at the edge could siginicantly improve content delivery, while latency can be reduced dramatically. Contents more widely distributed to the edge could guarantee flexibility and customisation on the network depending on user traffic demands	EDC
Communication services	Edge deployments of low-latency devices (compute and storage) for gamin,g AR, real-time ML to foundational radio access network (RAN) infrastructure and 5G services	Retailers are introducing more logistics, delivery, and recommendation intelligence to transform their businesses. Financial services institutions use automation and fraud detection to be more responsive to everything from online banking to underwriting and risk analysis	Edge gateways
Automated workflows	Automated data pipelines in event-driven architectures (Kafka)	Process automation	Event-driven archiecture
	New eventing technology (Knative in Kubernetes) that can spawn applications based on triggers, such as data updates. Even AI inferences that search for specific characteristics that trigger new applications and even feed the data back into an object repository	Automatic business rule enforcements, data synchronization	Eventing (knative in kubernets), AI/inference
	Federate data across sources and feed a pipeline for ML remodeling, creating a continuous improvement loop	Continuous improvement	Data federation

any data breach or component failure will not disable the ecosystem. Polices and rules are necessary in order to effectively utilize the newly introduced EDC, and even the local Edge layer computing and storage, preferably in some autonomous fashion. An orchestration and scheduling component is thus included in this reference architecture.

- **Cloud Datacenter Layer:** Here a conventional central DC is interconnected with multiple collaborative clouds. A database server is installed in the CDC, as well as the interconnected data centers across different cloud regions, together they act as the global data store for the ecosystem. Common cloud management functionality should be enhanced with rules/policies and scheduling mechanism that could facilitate the optimal use of the EDCs.

All the installed databases must be able to collaborate *as* a cohesive whole, replicating and synchronizing data captured at the edge across the rest of the ecosystem to guarantee that data is always available and never lost or corrupted. By spreading data processing across every layer of the architecture, greater speed, resilience, security and bandwidth efficiency can be achieved. For example, if the internet connection to the CDC slows or stops, applications can process data in the EDC and remains highly responsive. And if the cloud data center and edge data center become unavailable, applications with embedded databases continue to run as intended – and in real time – by processing and syncing data directly on and between devices. And if the catastrophic happens and all network layers become unavailable, edge devices with embedded data processing serve as their own micro data centers, running in isolation with 100% availability and real-time responsiveness until connectivity is restored.

This tiered approach insulates applications from central and regional data center outages. Each tier leverages increasingly local connectivity – which is more reliable – and synchronizes data within and across tiers. With such edge computing architecture, users and devices can always have fast access to data, no matter what exceptions could exist in the network systems.

Supplemental to the four horizontal layers, four vertical layers are added to address security, information, integration and governance of the entire system, providing a cohesive set of rules, regulations and services across the four fundamental layers:

- **The Security Layer** supports the establishment of cloud environments and secure infrastructures, platforms, and services across the entire ecosystem. It provides secure and dynamic development that prioritizes the design, development, and delivery of business services with necessary security enforcements and standardized baselines to evaluate the security of the offered services. It enumerates related security tools for monitoring, development, integration, risk assessment, and incident response in the edge computing environments. For many organizations, zero trust will be required for future expansion of the infrastructure and services.
- **The Information Layer** provides a unified information model and services provided by its IT services, applications, and systems. It covers the information architecture, business analytics and intelligence, metadata, and can be used as the basis for the creation of business analytics and intelligence. It also enables a virtualized information data layer, retrieving and transforming data from different sources into some mutually agreed common formats, and then exposing the data to consumers using different protocols and formats that support data consistency, and quality requirements.
- **The Integration Layer** is a key enabler that provides the capability to mediate the transformation, routing, and protocol conversion from various service requesters to the correct service providers, both with infrastructure and services. As the plumbing which interconnects all the collaborating system components, it facilitates the seamless access to services from other layers or providers, This layer enables the service consumer/requestor to connect to the correct service provider through the introduction of a reliable set of capabilities, with some well-designed "adapters".

- **The Governance Layer** ensures that the infrastructure and services a within an organization stick to the defined policies, guidelines, and standards that are defined as a function of the objectives, strategies, and regulations. It should conform to corporate, IT, and enterprise architecture governance principles and standards. Such a layer should include governance of processes for policy definition, management, and enforcement, as well as service and lifecycle governance, portfolio management, capacity and performance management, security, and monitoring.

3.2 A Proposed Service Model for the Edge

A reference architecture without well-defined set of infrastructure and business services is of no use. In Fig. 2, we propose a service model for the edge that can serve as the starting point for any organization that only need to tailor it for its own use.

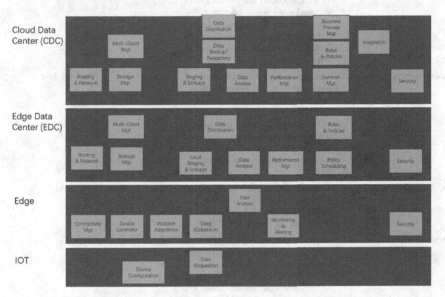

Fig. 2. Proposed service model for edge computing

Table 2 is a quick summary about each service:

4 Future of Edge Computing – Technology Imperative

4.1 Some Encouraging Trends

In this section, we quickly review some exciting trends that can make edge computing readily accepted and successful.

a) The responsibility for managing and securing edge solutions is shifting from line of business to corporate IT, as over 75% of CIOs now are responsible for IoT devices at the edge.

Table 2. Key services for edge computing

Service	Description	Layer	Core functionality
Device configuration	Some user or system-defined data sent from the Edge (with possible instructions from the EDC or CDC) to a device in order to better control the device. Such information should be persisted in Edge or EDC	IOT	Device Mgt
Data acquisition	While sensors generate/collect data, acquisition process that data into manageable sizes and convert it into digital formats. They also filter the data and select only vital information, reducing the amount to be processed and stored. Gateways transfer data over Wi-Fi, LANs or via internet. They can also work in the opposite direction, pulling commands from the cloud or distributing firmware updates. Network protection is critical at this stage as data is transferred	IOT & Edge	Data Mgt
Connectivity management	Manages connectivity with multiple types of services over wireless/cellular (2G, 3G, 4G/LTE and 5G), satellite, LPWA networks (3GPP and non-3GPP) and managed local or field-area networks (FANs), so to enable data collection and analysis. It also facilitates businesses to monitor, manage and control those devices	Edge	Network Mgt
Device controller	A collection of processes, tools, and technologies that help provision, monitor, and maintain the growing types and numbers of connected IOT devices	Edge	Device Mgt
Protocol adaptation	To provide compatibility between different types of IOT devices; and also between regular IP based networks and IoT comprised networks, as most of IoT comprised networks are low powered and resource constrained, therefore unable to process large size packets generated from regular networks	Edge	Data Mgt
Monitoring & alerting	A set of software (and hardware) components to provide surveillance over the existence and change of states and data/application flows in a system, in order to identify and eliminate potential faults. After possible failures are identified, alerting will notify the operators (management system or human-in-charge) to act upon the event to avoid catastrophic consequences	Edge	Device Mgt Data Mgt

(continued)

Table 2. (*continued*)

Service	Description	Layer	Core functionality
Data analytics & machine intelligence	To find trends, answers to what-if questions, and then draw patterns/insights/trends/conclusions or forecasts/predictions from analyzing both real-time and historical datasets with algorithms and specialized software. Such analytics could be descriptive, diagnostic, predictive, and prescriptive. Programs and software can also be developed that learn to make predictions and decisions without being directly programmed to do so. In general, the more information available, the more effective the analytics. Analytics can provide valuable and actionable outcomes and eventually help organizations plan for the future with better informed decisions	Edge EDC CDC	Analytics intelligence
Routing & network management	Routing is the process of selecting the best path using some predetermined rules with parameters specific to the equipment, network conditions, type of traffic, performance requirements etc. It creates efficiency in network communication and helps minimize network failure by managing data traffic so that a network can use as much of its capacity as possible without creating congestion. Network management is the process of administering and managing networks, including fault analysis, performance management, provisioning of networks/equipments such that desired quality of service can be achieved	EDC CDC	Network Mgt
Storage management	To manage large volume of data, both remote and on-premises storages across multi-layers need to be installed and managed across various cloud platforms. Typical management services include disaster recovery, backup, and long-term archiving	EDC CDC	Storage Mgt
Multi-cloud management	To monitor and secure applications and workloads across multiple cloud platforms and providers, both public and private	EDC CDC	Cloud Mgt

(*continued*)

Table 2. (*continued*)

Service	Description	Layer	Core functionality
Performance Mgt	Performance management examines the actual performance of hardware or a virtual system. It looks at things like system latency, signaling, CPU use, memory use, workload, etc. Applying this to the cloud means looking at how data moves from a client's office or other location across the Web and into a vendor's cloud storage systems. It also means looking at how that information is triaged and retrieved	EDC CDC	Cloud Mgt
Rules & policies	Policies allow you to define the way you want your users to behave in the cloud. They enable you to detect risky behavior, violations, or suspicious data points and activities in your cloud environment. If necessary, you can integrate remediation workflows to achieve complete risk mitigation. There are multiple types of policies that correlate to the different types of information you want to gather about your cloud environment and the types of remediation actions you may want to take	EDC CDC	Cloud Mgt
Policy-based scheduling & orchestration	Scheduling & Orchestration is the process of automating the tasks to manage connections and operations of workloads on private and public clouds. Such tasks include provision or start server workloads, provision storage capacity (if necessary), and instantiate virtual machines (VMs) by orchestrating services, workloads, and resources in the cloud. It can entail policy enforcement and ensure that processes have the proper permission to execute or connect to a workload	EDC CDC	Cloud/resource Mgt
Staging & linkage	The data staging process imports information either as streams or files, transforms them with complex calculations and cleansing, and produces integrated, cleansed data, then stages it for loading into data Stores or warehouses. Data linkage combines data from different sources that relate to the same person to create a new, enhanced data resource. This technique allows researchers to exploit and enhance existing data sources without the time and cost associated with primary data collection	EDC CDC	Data Mgt

(*continued*)

Table 2. (*continued*)

Service	Description	Layer	Core functionality
Data backup/repository	The practice of copying data from a primary data stores/storage to a secondary location, protecting them from disasters, accidents or malicious attacks	EDC CDC	Data Mgt
Data distribution	Data distribution service transfers large volume of data from the cloud to specific EDC or other edge devices and also among the edge servers themselves. Such operations can be expensive and some optimal data distribution strategy is necessary to minimize the cost of data distribution with proper delays. It integrates various components and services to provide low-latency data connectivity, extreme reliability, and a scalable architecture that business and mission-critical IOT applications need. The freedom and flexibility to deliver the data to different service. Key capabilities include: connectivity and application accessibility, indiscriminate data delivery, prioritized streaming data pipelines, and developer accessibility	EDC CDC	Data Mgt
Services Mgt	To plan, design, deliver, operate, and control all IT and cloud services that it offers to customers. It covers the operational aspects of applications and services, ensuring availability and performance per service level agreements (SLAs). It combines different software products and technologies into a cohesive management strategy that allows flexible and easy distribution of workloads between clouds while managing the costs	CDC	Business procee Mgt
Business process Mgt (BPM)	By incorporating advanced analytics, activity monitoring, and decision management capabilities, BPM enables organizations to discover, model, analyze, measure, improve and optimize their business strategy and processes/workflows with increased efficiencies and cost-savings. They have been particularly helpful in accelerating digital transformation	CDC	Business procee Mgt
Security	To protect users, sensitive data and services across the entire ecosystem, especially at the edge. It will protect data that lives or transports through devices out of centralized data centers	ALL	Security Mgt

b) The prevalence of smart devices themselves is projected to quadruple by 2025. This growth can dramatically expand the capabilities of edge computing, bringing about greater benefits such as lower latency, better efficiency and reduced costs. The further innovation and proliferation of IOT devices could also revolutionize various industries.

c) With reduced latency, organizations could provide optimal customer experience and generate more sales. A Deloitte study [3] found that a 100 ms improvement in mobile retail speeds translate to an 8.4% increase in sales conversion.

d) Spending has been exploding along with data generation, as MarketsandMarkets reported in October 2021 [4]. The edge computing market will grow from the already sizeable amount of $36.5 billion in 2021 to $87.3 billion by 2026, with a compound annual growth rate of 19% during those five years. The growing adoption of IoT across industries, exponentially increasing data volumes and network traffic and rising demand for low-latency processing and real-time, automated decision-making solutions are crucial factors that have been driving such phenomenal growth.

e) Increasingly edge has been expanding to distributed clouds, as the EDCs discussed before. Forrester Research [5] sees a growing presence of "data center marketplaces as a new edge hosting option," with organizations able to purchase compute space from smaller, local data centers in a cooperative marketplace aided by data center aggregators.

f) Telecommunications companies have an expanding role in the evolution of edge ecosystems, and they have been increasingly using their infrastructure that puts them physically close to nearly all potential customers. Telcos can offer both the edge computing infrastructure itself as well as supporting components, such as Secure Access Service Edge to support security in WAN and clouds. As 5G coverage further expands, and brings increasing speed and capacity to networks, organizations can harness both the low latency of edge computing and the speed of 5G to develop next-generation workloads and new use cases that rely on, or benefit from, the two technologies working in concert.

g) By 2027, machine learning (ML) in the form of deep learning (DL) will be included in over 65% of edge use cases, up from less than 10% in 2021 better efficiency and effectiveness in service delivery for businesses.

h) On the other hand, edge computing is seen as a threat to organizations, due to its increase of physical data sources and connected but insecure devices. If malicious attackers gain access to these devices, they could extract valuable information, tamper or destroy hardware, or even change entire operating systems and software. Clearly, cybersecurity is among the most common roadblocks faced when considering edge computing adoption and must take the forefront in the architecture process with zero-trust security and access policies.

As data isn't handled by a centralized system, secure access service edge (SASE) solution should be adopted that can address the governance issues. As a cloud-based cybersecurity service delivered directly to remote and edge devices instead of being hosted on a centralized enterprise data center, SASE provides identity-based and contextual security, in addition to enforcing your corporate data compliance policies. Such a robust solution would be able to regularly map new data sources, orchestrate security, and prevent vulnerabilities.

Visibility is the cornerstone of any edge security strategy. EC must discover and identify all devices across the ecosystem, apply the appropriate security policy, and quarantine them if necessary. All traffic to/from edge locations should be encrypted, and all (at least some sensitive) data in EDC of CDC should be stored encrypted.

i) Data sovereignty requirements and privacy and security regulations may dictate local storage and processing.

j) Many enterprise mission-critical applications need ultrareliable low-latency communications (URLLC) and massive machine type communications (mMTC) to connect a large number of devices in its service area. As expected, high-band solutions will only reach 50% coverage in the next 10 years, while low-band and midband 5G offerings similarly to 4G LTE continue to provide 80% of global coverage.

k) By 2025, reducing bandwidth cost will be the primary driver for new edge computing deployments, versus latency in 2021, as the cost of computing (Moore's Law) continue to drop, technologies to manage edge compute endpoints with zero touch becomes more mature.

4.2   Marching Toward Edge Computing

Organizations need to address many business and technical issues before they can turn edge computing into business growth opportunities. They must create their own extended infrastructure beyond the traditional cloud, and they had to consider where that infrastructure would live: on premises, in a private cloud, co-located, containerized? They had to consider the implications of a custom-built infrastructure's co-existence with public clouds. In addition, data at the edge and in IoT devices inherently exhibit problems with volume, latency, bandwidth, security and costs. If they built an edge data center in one location, how could they connect it to the cloud for centralized storage, and extend it to other locations as needed? And how could they ensure standardization and consistency of architectural components between locations, as well as redundancy and high availability? How could they distribute intelligence further out along the edge computing continuum that can address these issues in a more autonomous adaptive fashion? These sorts of questions made establishing an edge computing infrastructure a complex undertaking in its infancy.

We now present a list of key initiatives for every organization that want to move fast forward with edge computing so potential benefits could be realized.

Align Your Edge Device Infrastructure Mix with Business Needs: Edge computing is a massive technology category with potential use cases for nearly every industry, and for companies of any size. As always, any such technology breakthrough needs to be fully aligned with the business needs and the supporting organizational structure and process.

Architecture. Organizations need to make plans to capture the opportunities and prepare for the challenges of architecting, implementing, and deploying, managing the infrastructure, data and services in the vast edge environments. The best starting point to establish a sound and practical enterprise architecture [] that aligns business objectives with technology offerings such as infrastructure, services, and applications. Figure 1 is still only a high-level abstract reference architecture and Table 1 just presented a list of fundamental services without any design and implementation details, as they are not readily "instantiable or executable" yet. But they can serve as an excellent starting point, organizations can further develop them into finer grained, and even executable models.

Edge computing is the key to scale on Demand, while attempting to alleviate the ever-increasing demand for resources and performance with centralized infrastructure is quickly becoming prohibitively costly, infeasible and unmanageable. To cope with the ever-increasing need for volume and speed, the new architecture should be able to automatically provision and scale up or down on demand, with new resources such as network capacities, storage, and computing power as required. Such hyper scalability would help optimize the existing investments for edge deployments, ensuring that the landscape is ready for several thousand or even (theoretically) millions of devices and sensors.

In addition, reusable business services models, patterns and assets need to be defined, cataloged, and prioritized for development.

5G: With exceptional bandwidth and reliability, and very low latency, 5G fundamentally will change mobile communications, and elevate the adoption and performance of other technologies, especially IoT, cloud, and edge computing that open doors for exciting new business opportunities that are impossible before. 5G is highly reliable and can transmit data up to 100 times faster than 4G with latency close to zero, it provides stable connectivity that support devices that must work in real-time (such as security cameras, self-driving cars, oil mining fields, or robots used in remote surgery) to continue their operations without interruption even in remote environments. When billions of IoT devices communicate via 5G networks, data volume never seen before need to be transported and processed somewhere. Based on criticality or the computational power required, some of the data can be processed on the device itself, on the edge or cloud DCs or somewhere in between.

By opening the floodgates to edge computing, 5G localizes compute and storage, thereby reducing the consumption of expensive bandwidth because the devices only need to send that data that they cannot process by themselves to a central server or cloud. For example, enormous data could be generated from all the sensors in oil wells that cannot be processed locally as the sensors do not have enough computing power, so they process some data at the edge (in the sensors) and send the remaining to EDCs located in branch offices, and even the CDC at corporate HQs. Edge computing in this fashion will require large numbers of small, geographically dispersed EDCs, which may consist of as few as one or two hosts. Managing hundreds and sometimes thousands of these data centers will remain overwhelming.

5G deployment should also help standardize the implementation of 5G with high bandwidth as a minimum capability and minimum 3GPP specification version associated with coverage in the location. It is necessary to mandate service providers with guaranteed 5G coverage and bandwidth by defining the use case requirements and creating a minimum SLA with significant-enough penalties.

Machine Learning (ML)/Deep Learning (DL) and Inferencing: ML/DL at the edge can position edge devices as algorithmic or model-based intelligent data capture mechanisms, with the generated raw data transported up the layers for further upstream processing and analytics. ML at the edge can learn or uncover patterns otherwise hidden in the data, such as certain combination patterns from physical measurements that could predict failure of mechanical devices or diseases from patients. As such technology advances, specialized ML models (such as TensorFlow Lite Micro) can run on low-powered devices with limited computing and storage capacity, such as microcontroller units or even the sensors themselves.

Traditionally "hard coded" logic explicitly tells the edge system what to do under certain circumstances. Inferencing at the edge, however, can use richer datasets and conduct fast classification of inputs for the best possible processing – such as the confluence of events that predict a failure, with significantly improved responsiveness and analysis to the stream of data or sensor inputs.

Today, 99% of raw sensor data is discarded. By sensing and inferring at the edge, summaries of previously lost patterns, classifications and anomalies can be quickly created and transported to upper layer processing, saving the resources needed to upload the original data.

Inferencing requires GPUs or high-performance CPUs with enough computing power to run the models and made such capabilities infeasible at the device edge. Emerging neuromorphic technologies promise significant improvement in inference speed and power consumption at the edge. Advancements in model optimization already allow true inferencing to take place in devices as common and low cost/low power as Arduino (and compatible MCUs). In addition, recent models such as TensorFlow Lite and TensorFlow Lite Micro can address such problems based on mathematic models and algorithms. Today inference with DL can be run truly at the edge, with widespread edge-based training upcoming soon.

Performance Monitoring and Control: Edge computing encompasses many different types of IOT devices and millions of such devices could be there working together on-location. All those devices connecting to the edge network needs to be actively discovered and identified by monitoring connectivity, together with management and diagnostic capabilities such as measuring resource utilization (data storage, network bandwidth, CPU usage, etc.) broken down by services and applications. Some access policy is also imperative, placing, for example, all unknown devices into quarantine.

Failures will happen because of network partitions or infrastructure outages, especially node/pod failures that are common at the far edge. Applications and databases should be designed for their appropriate operating modes. The cloud runs in mostly connected mode (though the impact of a cloud outage can be severe). Near-edge applications should be in the most connected or semi-connected mode, the latter of which could provide an extended network partition that lasts several hours. Applications at the far edge should be designed for semi-connected or disconnected mode, in which they run independently of any external site.

Securing the Edge: It has been challenging to monitor, manage and protect the increasingly more complex network environments, shift to edge computing make things much more difficult. As organizations are adopting new approaches and emerging security solutions, they still need legacy controls, such as: firewall at network edge, intrusion and threat detection, data leakage monitoring, device authentication and network access restrictions (device-to-device), and application proxy (e.g., secure web gateway, CASB, etc.).

The distributed nature of edge computing increases the attack surface. It's important to consider applying least-privilege practices throughout and zero-trust security. Other essential factors include encryption both in transit and at rest, multi-tenancy support at the database layer and per-tenant encryption, and the regional locality of data to ensure compliance.

All security measures should also undergo penetration tests to ensure they're working properly; any weaknesses can be identified and dealt-with early.

AI/ML can be useful to comprehend the collected data, identify patterns and deviations from those patterns, therefore detect and respond to potential failures or threats. For example, AI/ML can be used in threat intelligence to create malware clusters that can detect and predict the behaviors of malware families, eventually speeding up the detections of malware variations within those families. It can be used for User Entity Behavior Analytics (UEBA), detecting anomalies in user/entity behavior on the network. These tools augment or supplement what the security practitioner is doing, thereby creating faster detection of anomalies, and freeing up that practitioner to focus on other, more strategic tasks or higher-level work.

AL/ML could also play an important role in access management and enforcement control to support risk and trust decision-making related to users and devices trying to access applications, workloads, or other devices. For enhanced security at the edge, enterprises should prioritize the adoption of the zero-trust architecture. Therefore, when a user logs into a system, it not only asks for a username and password but also monitors what kind of computer you have, the software, etc. so that they know the user is who they say tey are. Additionally, this gives the user limited access to data, allowing protection for the rest of the company's data in case of a breach. Zero Trust environments facilitate continuous, dynamic risk and trust testing based on external security information, security policy, state of the network, identity, the request beings made, and threat intelligence.

Use edge topology to address data sovereignty and availability requirements while minimizing risk by extending data and analytics governance capabilities to edge environments and providing visibility through active metadata.

Automated Workflows: With the pattern-based event-driven architectures and sensors on-location, business workflows across many industries (manufacturing, financial services, healthcare, telecommunications, and entertainment etc.) can be automated that eventually lead to improved operations and, in many cases, benefiting the lives of people. For example, to enable preventative maintenance, tolerances from sensors, such as vibrations or temperature, are monitored. When a device goes out of tolerance, the workflow will automatically notify factory personnel of potential issues.

Organizations can start to create edge-validated patterns and reusable assets such as business use cases with workflows, blueprints, code repositories. A framework should be established or adopted that makes it easier to create new patterns, while reusing or enhancing existing patterns. And since the pattern is reproducible, it can be scaled as required, repeatable for other organizations, modified for differentiation and extended for different workloads and use cases.

Distributed Data Processing: Distributed processing can improve reliability as well as the user experience. Data persistence in edge environments should include edge-resident relational and nonrelational database management systems (DBMSs), and small-footprint-embedded databases for storage and processing of data closer to or even inside the edge devices. Such distributed data architectures optimize by balancing the latency requirements against the need for data consistency between cloud/data center and the edge, as well as across edge environments. They also address issues related to the scalability, latency, geo-distribution, productivity, and security needs of edge applications.

Distributed SQL is an emerging class of DBMS that provides a versatile and powerful data layer that can run across different tiers of the cloud and edge, and matches well for the edge data layer, as it combines the best features of traditional RDBMSs and NoSQL databases for running transactional applications in edge computing environments. With distributed SQL resiliency, data is replicated across tiers and servers, keeping services available during node, zone, region and data center failures, thus it is resilient **with** no single points of failures. Database clusters thus created can be scaled **horizontally** on demand. A distributed SQL database offers synchronous and asynchronous replication within a DC (wither CDC or EDC), and between the DCs and the edge. A well-designed distributed SQL database also bolsters security with encryption on both stored and in-transit data, multi-tenancy support at the database layer and per-tenant encryption and regional locality of data to ensure compliance.

Stateful Edge Applications: New edge applications exploit devices and network gateways to perform tasks and provide services locally on behalf of the cloud—with the most powerful edge applications being stateful. Stateful edge computing means that such applications can continue to function without disruption in case of failures somewhere in the system. These applications will be composed of multiple autonomous services all working independently with local data, where services can communicate with each other at the edge directly, or in a point-to-point fashion. They are not dependent on an always-on connectivity back to the CDC or even the EDC (so-called local-first cooperation). This will result in systems could be extremely resilient, run 24/7 without stopping and that can adaptively detect, react to, and cope with failure of some of the components or services. Applications of this nature include emergency services, trading systems, manufacturing IoT systems, and autonomous vehicles, etc.

However, stateful edge applications demand a new data architecture that considers the scale, latency, availability, and security needs of the applications. There remains a need for a software-defined storage addition that can support the protection and management of valuable data at the edge with a high degree of automation, together with robust data persistency and always-on availability.

Metaverse: As Mark Zuckerberg emphasized,"Creating a true sense of presence in virtual worlds delivered to smart glasses and VR headsets will require massive advances in connectivity. Bigger than any of the step changes we've seen before."[] Edge computing can help solve this problem. With compute and storage capacity placed closer to metaverse participants, Edge computing supports the metaverse by minimizing network latency, reducing bandwidth requirements, and storing most of the data locally, while such systems can generally work in conjunction with a cloud system when network connections are available.

Organizational Issues: Most business applications have been managed by line of business (LOB). As organizations start to innovate such applications with new technology, it is usually the LOB that drives the advancement without much buy-in or governance from corporate technology authorities. However, as discussed before, edge computing calls for unified architecture for information, and services (both technical and business), and infrastructure, in order to make on-demand placements of data, services close to the source of data or actions. LOB owned IT/OT will need to be transitioned to the corporate IT/OT, and this may introduce significant realignments, in terms of both the organizational structure and the supporting business processes.

Data management strategy needs to be augmented with distributed processing capability, including edge data persistence, integration, governance, and analytics. To ensure efficient and effective deep learning at the edge, organizations must include edge in any enterprise AI/ML effort, and share experience, skills, models and services.

To maximize the success of edge computing solutions, organizations need to invest in skills development that ensures collaboration between OT and data management teams in IT. Critical skillsets that facilitate the rapid innovation on new solutions to the issues raised in this section would continue to be critical and in high demands.

5 Conclusion

This paper first reviewed the evolution from cloud computing to edge computing, the driving forces behind and the potential benefits. Business necessity for such evolution is presented as a list business use cases are summarized with scenarios, benefits, and key enablers, with many on the list fully or partially in operation in in development. Then a proposed tiered (layered) reference architecture, augmented with critical vertical layers of security, information, integration, and governance that provide unified architectural components, frameworks, and reusable assets across all the horizontal tiers. Finally, after summarizing a long list of exciting trends for advancing and adopting edge computing, a set of critical issues or future work is presented that should get the attention from both the academic and industry edge (and cloud) computing community.

References[1]

1. Gartner: What edge computing means for infrastructure and operations leaders (2018). https://www.gartner.com
2. IDC: Expect 175 zettabytes of data worldwide by 2025. Network World (2016)
3. Deloitte: Milliseconds make millions (2020). https://www2.deloitte.com/in/en.html
4. Markets and Markets: Edge computing market worth $101.3 billion by 2027 (2022)
5. Forrester: Predictions 2021: edge computing hits an inflection point (2021). https://www.forrester.com/bold

[1] I intentionally removed most (over 70) of the references I should include normally, as this paper emphasized on some fundamental principles, use cases, architecture and services. Enlisting all of them here will not offer too much more help.

Author Index

Printed in the United States
by Baker & Taylor Publisher Services